From BAREFOOT to STILETTOS,

It's not for sissies

A MEMOIR BY

MARIE PIZANO

BALBOA.
PRESS

A DIVISION OF HAY HOUSE

Cover and Chapter page artwork by Michael P Maness
Cover Graphic Design by Nick Barron
Cover photo by Hal Jaffe of Jaffe Studio
Cover Graphic Design touch up by Elaine Koger of Murals of Memphis
Author photo by Donna Criswell of Key to Life Photography

Balboa Press books may be ordered through booksellers or by contacting:

Balboa Press
A Division of Hay House
1663 Liberty Drive
Bloomington, IN 47403
www.balboapress.com
1 (877) 407-4847

Printed in the United States of America.

ISBN: 978-1-4525-8668-7 (sc)
ISBN: 978-1-4525-8669-4 (hc)
ISBN: 978-1-4525-8666-3 (e)

Library of Congress Control Number: 2013920730

Balboa Press rev. date: 12/10/2013

Contents

A portion of the proceeds from this book is donated to The Exodus Foundation, Inc., a public awareness organization whose **vision** is to eradicate the widespread epidemic of domestic violence. The **mission** of The Exodus Foundation, Inc. is to assist victims of domestic violence by providing essential emergency services needed to transition clients from victims to survivors. The **goal** of The Exodus Foundation, Inc. is to increase public awareness of and involvement in domestic violence issues. The Exodus Foundation, Inc. is a nonprofit 501 (c)(3) organization providing assistance and referral services to victims and survivors of domestic violence. Their focus is to provide an emergency shelter for victims who have escaped their abuser and seek a safe-haven. For more information visit http://www.exodusfoundationdv.org.

They say that there are three sides to every story: your side, my side, and the truth.

This is my healing. This is my story. This is my truth.

Most importantly of all, this is... my FORGIVENESS.

This book is dedicated to my true soul mates, my children, may you always find your "YES"

Acknowledgments

Producing this book took the many hours and talents of many of my highly skilled friends to whom I am deeply appreciative of their commitment to the task and for their belief in me. I thank them, and many others, for also giving me the inspiration and courage to write this book.

Whitney Johnson, the Ghostwriter, I am grateful for the commitment and dedication you gave while helping me write this book. For your loyalty, friendship, protectiveness and perfection, thank you. To Jocelyn Regenwether, my editor, my new friend.

My Children, my true soul mates, for your unconditional love and patience and showing me what the meaning of life is all about. You two are the main reason I enjoy each and every day.

My parents, my Mom, my Dad, you have taught me so much and made me feel loved and secure, even at the worst moments when life has thrown me that curve ball. I hope you truly know how much I appreciate all the struggles you went through for us. I am forever thankful, I am forever blessed to have you both in my life. I am grateful for your courage and the values you have taught me.

My Grandparents, I miss you and even though you are not on this earth, I know you are always watching over me and my children. I said it to you while you were here and I will say it again for all to

know; thank you for all your knowledge, strength, solid foundation and mostly the love I received from the both of you.

My ex-husband, it may be strange to say, and bittersweet, but you have made me fight for independence and be stronger than I could ever imagine and you have brought out the worst and the best in me. You pushed me to really discover Me. I am forever thankful for your participation in making it possible for me to become a mother. Although it was tough, I have truly learned forgiveness from our experiences and I am glad we found our peace.

Michael P. Maness, for your friendship and your incredible talent you have shared for this book. For your insights and advice. You're an inspiration to many and I am blessed to call you my friend. I thank you for always believing in me and watching out for me.

Hal Jaffe, your talent amazes me. Thank you for your time and talent to help produce a photo that I am proud of showing to the world. Thank you for being my friend.

To Roxie Willis and my team, to all those who stand by me, advise me and who help me build this empire, thank you for believing and for the time you give towards this dream, your friendship is what gets me through the tough times. I am forever appreciative and grateful for everything. My mentor, advisor and dear friend, Richard Sandor, you are the ultimate Rock Star!

To Tom Taylor (Chopper) and his wife Courtney for allowing me the use of their motorcycle for the cover photo. To Robin Cooper, for your inspiration and courage to help others.

Legal Disclaimer

In this book the author repeatedly states **her opinion** of her belief that all the many references are telling the truth, and the author is expressing her **personal opinions.** The author believes that the many "proofs of guilt" and "consciousness of guilt's" described within are factually true, but in any event they represent her **personal opinions**. The author is expressing **her own personal opinions** regarding her feelings about her life story and present what she believes is true to the best of her knowledge, it remains **her personal opinion**. The reader can make their own decision as to the relative validity of the author's comments, sources, her conclusions and **her personal opinions**.

General Disclaimer: THE INFORMATION PRESENTED HEREIN IS PROVIDED "AS-IS" AND WITHOUT WARRANTY OF ANY KIND, EITHER EXPRESS OR IMPLIED INCLUDING, BUT NOT LIMITED TO, WARRANTIES OF FITNESS FOR A PARTICULAR PURPOSE, MERCHANTABILITY, OR FREEDOM FROM INFRINGEMENT OF PATENT, TRADEMARK, OR COPYRIGHT. The author of this information shall not be liable for any incidental or consequential damages for injuries arising out of the use of the information presented herein. The information presented herein may be protected by United States and/or foreign patents and/or copyrights, which may or may not be owned or licensed by the author. Any and all brand names and/or product names which may be used herein are the intellectual property of their respective owners. No copyright claim is made to original U.S. Government works, if any, contained herein. The viewing or use of the information presented herein does not grant an express or implied license to commercially use or republish any such information. By using or accessing any of the information presented herein, reader/user hereby agrees to be personally liable and to fully indemnify author, his family, members, employees, agents, web site hosts, internet service providers, heirs and assigns for any and all damages directly and/or consequentially resulting from such use or attempted use of this information, alone or with, or under the authority of, any other persons, including, without limitation, any governmental agencies, wherein such damages include without limitation, damages resulting from loss of revenue and/or property, fines, and attorney's fees, including, without limitation, those generated by prosecution and/or governmentally imposed seizures, forfeitures, and/or injunctions. This Disclaimer shall be governed by the laws of the State of Tennessee, exclusive of any choice of law provisions which would require the application of the laws of another jurisdiction. All disputes and matters whatsoever arising under, in connection with, or incident to this Disclaimer and/or any information presented herein shall be litigated, if at all, in and before a Court of competent jurisdiction located in Tennessee. County in the State of Tennessee, United States of America, to the exclusion of the Courts of any other state or country. This author makes no representation that the information presented in this book and/other is appropriate or available for use in other jurisdictions, and access of this information from jurisdictions where its contents are illegal is prohibited. Readers/users accessing this information from other jurisdictions do so on their own initiative and are responsible for compliance with the applicable laws of that jurisdiction. This author reserves the right, at his/her sole discretion, to modify this Disclaimer in any manner and from time to time, without prior notice. The terms of any such amendment to this Disclaimer shall become effective immediately upon posting of such terms, and reader/user's access of this information on or after such posting shall constitute acceptance of such amended terms. The Summary, headings and captions of this Disclaimer are inserted for reference convenience and do not define, limit or describe the scope or intent of this Disclaimer or any particular section, paragraph or provision. Pronouns and nouns shall refer to the masculine, feminine, neuter, singular or plural, as the context shall require. The information presented herein is for informational purposes only. Should any portion of this Disclaimer be found or declared null and void for any reason whatsoever, all other portions shall remain in full force and effect.

In closing, you understand that this book is not intended as a substitute for consultation with a licensed medical, educational, legal or accounting professional. Before you begin any change in your lifestyle in any way, you will consult a licensed professional to ensure that you are doing what's best for your situation.

This book provides content that relates to the authors personal story. The author has the right according to the First Amendment. As such, the purchase and use of this book implies your acceptance of this disclaimer.

Foreword:

Titanium Stilettos

Foreword: Titanium Stilettos

From Barefoot to Stilettos is a memoir written with the hope to inspire and empower the inner warrior in each of us, dedicated to reminding us to walk tall each and every day, regardless of what we're up against.

I have always regarded stilettos as a symbol of power, poise and perseverance. I tell everyone that my own stilettos are made and reinforced with titanium, a metal characterized by a high melting point, resistance to corrosion, and the highest strength-to-weight ratio of any metal on earth – in other words, composed to withstand the utmost pressure.

Repeatedly, my stilettos have proven their capacity to carry me through every trial, every storm, and every fire yet still emerge unscathed and ready to carry me another day. My journey thus far has taught me that any "no" that this life attempts to deliver to me is not a conclusion, but merely a hurdle. In my titanium stilettos rest the strength and power to kick in as many doors as it takes to get to my "yes."

Through explorations of my own past and present tense, my desire is to encourage self-reflection about how the sum of our experiences – for better or for worse – should be bringing us closer to the futures, the selves, the lives, and the destinations that we envision and deserve.

This is for the women and for anyone who knows that no one else can fill your stilettos – yet also for those still living on the other side of that reality, still searching for the perfect pair, still stumbling as they work to perfect their stride.

It is a privilege and an honor to strut in our stilettos, to fight in them, to conquer in them day in and day out. But I know, firsthand, that the journey from barefoot to stilettos is not for sissies. They are, indeed, tough shoes to fill. So the truth is, we all stumble in them from time to time. The truth is, that's perfectly all right. Truth is, within each of us is the power, poise and perseverance to pick ourselves back up to walk tall another day.

This book is dedicated to making sure that none of us ever forget that.

Chapter 1:
Blood of Survivors

Chapter 1: Blood of Survivors

My family is one made up of fighters – people who've never understood the meaning of "no," "can't," "stop," "limits," or "impossible."

During World War II, my grandfather and his comrades dug holes with their bare hands and buried themselves in the sand to avoid attack by enemy tanks. The tanks rolled over them in their hiding places, and he and one other soldier were the only two to survive that encounter. The worst consequence that my grandfather suffered from that experience was painful arthritis for the rest of his life. At another point – not sure whether this was during the war or sometime else – my grandfather was shot in the head, but he survived that too, suffering only a scar and a plate in his head.

My grandfather had fled to America from Italy. From what I was told, his escape had something to do with his parents being shot by his best friend over land, and even more to do with being next on that hit list. So from the little bit I understand, he had to get out of that country, and he had to get out of there fast.

He escaped to Mexico first and then traveled to the United States – a path I'll never understand given that he'd have bypassed the U.S. to get to Mexico. I never got the complete picture why he chose the route to Mexico first, but that would explain the make-up of my Italian-Mexican-American family.

He was around 36 years old and my grandmother was around the age of 13 when he met her in America and courted her briefly before offering her Mexican family a dowry of cows in exchange for her hand in marriage. As a result, the nature of their relationship was that he essentially became her father and her husband at once. She married so young, but immediately started having all these babies. I never understood her utter strength until I was all grown up.

My grandfather was my world from the start. I idolized him so much that when I got a little older, I even tried to learn to shave like him. He liked his shave the old-fashioned way – mixing the cream in the shaving cup, and then brushing it onto his face and shaving the hair away with a knife. When I got old enough to start shaving my legs, I went about it exactly the way my grandfather did his shaving.

I was with him during his final days, although, for some reason, my uncles didn't want me around at the hospital. He always used to tell me that I was his favorite, and my grandmother would get upset with him for spending so much more time with me than with his other grandchildren. When he saw me from behind the mask he had to wear, his eyes would light up, and my grandmother would say, "Well, he knows Marie is here!" Still, my uncles were constantly ushering me out of the room.

One uncle, who I felt was particularly jealous, hardened, and controlling, was always trying to put me in my place. I couldn't understand why he treated me like such an outcast, since he was the one with a history of doing wrong by my grandparents, but I learned from him during my grandfather's final days the necessity of considering the source. I had to realize that, no matter what he tried to take from me or the rest of our family, I had my grandfather's love and that was all that mattered. I wasn't going to let my uncle break

3

me down because of his misery. My mother made sure of that, too. She had always stood her ground with her brothers throughout life and instilled in me the strength to not to take any crap from them or any man, no matter who he might be. In those days, I just shrugged him off and tried to focus on what mattered.

In the few moments I did get to spend alone with my grandfather before he passed away, I made sure I told him what a wonderful man he had been, how special he was to me, and that I would remember him forever.

So many things about my grandfather remain a mystery to me. For some reason, he has two separate birth certificates, so my family never knew his real age. Every time he told me about his life, his stories grew bigger and bigger – altogether, his tales have led me to believe that either he made it all up, or he had nine lives. In any case, he was truly a tough guy. For all his adventures, he was somewhere in his late 90's by the time he passed away of natural causes. Regardless of how much truth or exaggeration fueled his tall tales, they laid the groundwork for the legacy I had to live up to. His imperturbable strength and his unbreakable spirit made him my idol.

Once he was gone, I realized that he had been my world, and I didn't even have any pictures of him. All that I had left of him was his 48-star American flag he'd given me from World War II – and the blood of survivors pumping through my veins.

And how could I, with that gift from him, learn to ever take no for an answer?

Chapter 2:

Becoming MVP

Chapter 2: Becoming MVP

Probably a little too understanding of the plights facing immigrants heading to America, my grandfather used to take in people from overseas and hide them in the attic until they received their American citizenship. As a matter of caution, he had always told my mother when she was young never to go into the attic.

Well, she went snooping anyway, as little girls do. From what I understand, she inevitably was curious to learn what it was she wasn't supposed see in this enticingly forbidden attic. She wound up being sexually abused by one of the boarders.

One way or another, Grandpa had that guy "taken care of." It's not for me or anyone else to say whether he got the man deported, or whether he took matters into his own hands and issued his own brand of punishment. All I've gathered, from what I've been told is that the man was never seen or heard from again after that.

Years later, regarding that incident, my mother spoke to a reporter about the molestation as her inspiration for heading up a non-profit chapter in her city, to help missing and abused children. Her words? "The way I see it, there are two roads you can take. You can play victim, or you can do something about it. So I chose to pick up my panties and move on and go do something about it." As soon as she had spoken those words, she had given them to me to live by. It is by those words that I like to characterize my mother, her unyielding strength and her insatiable resolve.

After all my grandmother's sons joined the military, one by one, and were scattered all over the world – one in Hawaii, one in Japan, one in Vietnam – she was so overwhelmed with worry that she had a nervous breakdown. To ease my grandmother's load, my mom had to take over a lot of responsibilities at a young age. Then, suddenly, my grandfather decided he wanted to marry her off to a 40-year-old man.

My mother wasn't having it. It was the 1960's, she was an artist, she had dreams, and she had already sacrificed so much. She was not about to allow any old overbearing, father-appointed husband to get in the way of the life she had envisioned for herself. Tired of taking care of everyone, and determined not to have her destiny outlined by my grandfather, she ran off, did not marry that man and moved in with her cool, hip Aunt Jenny.

After that, she met an Italian man who had a Don Juan flair she couldn't resist. She moved in with him long enough for him to become my "sperm donor," which is what I call him since that's all he ever amounted to as far as my life was concerned. The man that I consider to be my father came along much later.

When the "sperm donor" found out that my mom was pregnant, he swore up and down that I wasn't his. My devastated mother had already been deprived of her own childhood as a baby raising babies, her siblings. Now she was about to have me – and apparently, alone.

There was no way my mother was going back home then. My grandfather was outraged over just about everything she had done by this point, beginning with refusing to live out the life expected of her and marrying the 40-year-old fellow chosen for her. He didn't like that she'd fled her familial ties, and that she was so wild and free. Now he certainly didn't like that she was pregnant.

So after "sperm donor" rejected the responsibility of fatherhood, my mother moved in with her best friend, a heavy-set woman who had an uncanny resemblance to Nell Carter from that 1980s sitcom, *Gimme a Break!* Grandpa didn't like her either, mainly because he felt she was the cause of my mothers rebellious behavior.

I was born in Cook County Hospital in Chicago, with jaundice, bronchitis, and plenty of other health issues. I grew up as Marie Valentina Pizano, but on the day I was born, as I found out from my mother much later in life, she had actually named me after her friend – the one who resembled Nell Carter.

My grandfather was furious! When he found out what my mother had named me, he was so irate that he burst into the hospital and started barking orders at the nurses and everybody in sight. He declared to my mother that we were coming with him, and he demanded to the nurses that they change the name on my birth certificate. No one argued with the snarling man giving commands in his thick, intimidating Italian-Mexican accent.

My grandfather combined the name of a saint for my first name with what was supposed to be the first name of my grandmother, Balentina, for my middle name, but the anxious nurse didn't understand my grandfather's accent and clearly didn't care to provoke any further wrath with her questions and confusion. She had already apparently been so shaken up by my grandfather's fury that she'd first typed her own last name (Lopez) onto the birth certificate by accident. So she did the best she could with the spelling, and by the time all was finally said and done, I had become Marie Valentina Pizano, the family's original MVP.

I never knew a thing about any of this until I was 28 years old and needed my birth certificate in order to get a passport for my honeymoon. I was waiting for my name to be called and heard over the loudspeaker, "Marie Valentina Lopez Pizano." I went to the counter, looked at the certificate and said without even thinking, "Now, who the fuck is Lopez?!"

It was crazy enough that I had some mysterious Italian "sperm donor" roaming around out there somewhere in the world, someone who could claim me as his own but whom I would never recognize if he was staring me right in the face – but his last name was certainly not Lopez! Instantly, a vision flashed into my thoughts, of my mother riding around free and wild on the back of a motorcycle with some huge Mexican biker. You never knew with my mother.

If that wasn't enough for me to try and figure out, when the guy handed me my birth certificate, I saw that it also contained another name (the one my mother had given me originally but had never spoken a word to me about!) with several x's marked through the letters – I suppose because there was no correction tape or white-out way back when I was born.

So I yelped, "That's not even my name!" and demanded to know, as if this poor guy behind the desk was the guy with all the answers, "Who is this other person's name on my birth certificate?!" The guy just stared at me blankly and finally asked, "Are your parents still alive? Maybe you can ask them." Oh yeah, my mother got a phone call, all right! Only after all that commotion did I finally learn the whole history.

So even my birth wasn't one for sissies – pure chaos culminating into a hell of a name that I certainly had no choice but to live up to!

Chapter 3:

Harsh Realities

Chapter 3: Harsh Realities

When I was about two years old the "sperm donor" showed up at my grandparents' door wanting to see me and my mom. It never happened because my grandfather grabbed his gun and told the guy to get off his property, and fast. When he didn't leave, my grandfather started shooting at the ground, telling him, "You denied her once. You'll never deny her again." Grandfather told him he didn't have the right to see my mother or to claim me – that he was never welcome to come around again. This event gave me my earliest lesson from my grandfather, that you do the right thing in this life from the beginning, or else! There are consequences for the choices we make, whether they be good or bad.

There was no other way it could have or should have gone down – because from the very beginning, see, that's what we Pizanos were all about: picking up our panties and moving on. My mother and I had each other, and we had my grandparents, and we were happy with just that much. It was more than enough for us. The "sperm donor" was dead weight – someone we did not need or want.

It was also around that same time when my mother met this man who fathered my little sister. All I remember is that there was my mom, there was me… and then all of a sudden came this man and my sister right afterward. This man married my mother not long after my sister was born, but it didn't last long. They had too many problems and fought all the time, until it eventually became unbearable for my mom.

Briefly, we all lived together in a high rise off of Lake Shore Drive. There are very few fond memories of that time. I remember this man, the one who was my sisters father, bought me a fish tank full of goldfish and angelfish – and that's about the only good memory of him that I recall.

I always felt fear in his presence because he always seemed so angry, but I always felt safe in my mother's arms. When she was around, I knew nothing would hurt me. He was always drunk, and his own parents were miserable and unpleasant – his father, a tyrant, and his mother, a wretch who, as I recall, always made horrible comments about my mom while babysitting me.

On one occasion, when my sister and I were at his parents' house while my mother was at work, his mother shoved soap in my mouth after I had repeated a word her husband had said, which was "Fuck!" I hadn't even understood the word. I had just heard it so much when I was around them that, when I said it, I couldn't understand why I was forced to choke on soap for it.

To this day, if I ever see or hear of people making a child eat soap as a punishment, I swear I will kick them extra hard with my stilettos. I never understood who came up with that punishment. In my book, it's child abuse, plain and simple! I remember crying and feeling scared and confused the entire time I waited for my mother to pick me up and take me home. When she came back and heard what happened, all hell broke loose. She swore on everything that they would never get away with that or see me ever again.

It wasn't a good situation for anyone involved – not for me, my mother, or my sister. But in the meantime, the reality was that my mother had a child with him, and I now had a sister who was like a real life baby-doll that I adored and couldn't imagine my life without.

I was young, so the details of everything that was happening were beyond me. All that I remember was that one night he was coming after my mother, viciously angry over who knows what, so she took one of his beer bottles and hit him over the head to stop him. After that night, it was pretty clear to my mother that we needed to pack up and get out. But every time my mom tried to leave, he became abusive.

I remember coming home one night to what looked like a cross between the aftermath of a raid by villainous burglars and a scene from the movie *Animal House*. The couches were ripped up, glasses were broken, empty beer cans were scattered on the floor, clothes were tossed everywhere, furniture was toppled over, file cabinets were thrown open, and papers were strewn all over the apartment.

My mom had told him she was ready to leave him, but he didn't want her to go and certainly not with his child. She left with me and my sister anyway. Anytime we managed to move, he would find out where we were living and then break in and tear the place apart.

He and his family made it clear that we weren't taking my sister with us anywhere. His parents refused to accept that their son was an abuser. Instead, they blamed my mother for any problems he had and they helped him take her to court and somehow win their custody battle.

No one won, the way I see it. The whole ordeal gave me my first lesson in the harsh reality that there are always so many sides to each and every story – and that, unfortunately, the truest or noblest versions do not always prevail.

Chapter 4:

Only Child Syndrome

Chapter 4: Only Child Syndrome

It was the hardest thing in the world for my mother, allowing someone to take her child away. For me, it felt like my little sister was taken out of my life just as quickly as she had come into it. We got occasional visits with her, but how could that be enough?

My mother had the weight of the world on her shoulders, and the battles she had faced so far had not been easy ones for her to fight. Now she had to figure out how to move forward alone. It took me years to comprehend the strength it must have required for her to keep everything together and provide for herself and a daughter.

I remember seeing her pay for our groceries with food stamps and noticing that the money looked different from the dollar or two I got every once in a while to spend on Lake Shore Drive. I wondered why the grocery money looked different from the other money even though we seemed to use them the same way. I thought it meant that we were special, like royalty, for being able to use a different kind of money. I always had what I needed, so it never occurred to me at that age that we were poor in the eyes of society.

By the time I was almost five years old, I was left to live with my grandparents while my mother decided to go on a quest for greener pastures. She still had a wild streak, having learned street smarts while hanging around and riding with a motorcycle gang. For years, she had wanted to move to California and become an artist, and now she felt like it was about damn time. She had yet to be able to choose to live the life that she'd wanted, and it hadn't stopped nagging at her.

So there she wound up, on the back of a buddy's bike one night, California-bound, but just like that, she encountered a force that stopped her in her tracks.

During a stop for drinks at a tavern in South Deering, Illinois, my mother met a man who told her that she wasn't going to California – that she was staying there, with him. And he was right. When her friend's bike rode off again from the bar, she wasn't on the back of it. She stayed behind and had a couple more drinks with the fellow she'd met instead.

I will forever be thankful that she did – because that night, that meeting with him, led to the introduction of the man I proudly claim as my Father, my Dad.

When I first met him, I did not like him one bit. He seemed nice enough, but I wasn't keen on him having my mother's attention. I didn't like him appearing out of nowhere and invading my space with her, so I gave him hell every chance I got. It was nothing personal, really. I had just gotten used to having my mother all to myself and hated sharing her with anyone. But within something like a year, he had moved in with us and later become her husband and my Dad, in the truest sense of both words.

My dad's mother lived in what are called "project homes" – low income, almost poverty-level apartment complexes. Surrounding the area were several gangs. Where my grandmother lived was somewhat of a safe zone, a neutral ground. The gangs had claimed their turf around the apartment complexes, and gang members were not allowed to enter the others without some kind of consequence. During my summer vacations, I would visit my grandmother and stay with her for a couple of weeks. My grandmother was adored by the neighborhood kids; she was kind to them and would often share a cigarette or food with them. As I got to learn the neighborhood and meet people who lived around there, I began to get the sense that they protected my grandmother. When I would visit and sit out front on the bench, I would witness many gang-related activities, and I learned from the neighbors a sense of "street smarts" just from being around them and listening to the stories they told about their lives. One particular young mother I met, about 16 years old, was in a gang. She was one of the neighbors who really liked my grandmother. She basically took me under her wing, and every time I would visit, I would hang out with her and she would protect me from any harm. She was good to me. I did, however, witness an initiation into her gang, and I learned what happens to people when they don't follow the rules. I think it was one of the most intriguing, yet terrifying, things I have witnessed. I saw her carve her initials into the other girl's forehead as a punishment, a reminder not to forget who she was, after the other girl was found messing around with her boyfriend. I learned many things from these neighbors, about how each of their struggles defined who they were and why they lived there. It was definitely a harsh reality check of what living in poverty and around gangs was all about. My dad tried to get his mother to move out of that area, but she was very content living there.

Not long after my parents married, I can recall one time visiting my grandmother, and while my parents and I sat around the breakfast table, I started demanding that I wanted siblings. They talked about it, but that wasn't enough. I commanded that they give me a brother or sister. The sister I'd had and adored once upon a time had been snatched away from me – clearly, by my youthful logic, the most feasible solution was for them to make another little baby.

They assured me, "Well, maybe someday."

Not good enough.

I insisted, in my classic MVP style, "No. I want one now!"

If they weren't going to fulfill my wish for me, I'd just have to handle it myself. I wanted a little sister or brother, and dammit, I was going to have one.

One hot summer day, while we were visiting my grandmother (on my Dad's side), I went outside to play with the friends I had made. We were on the sidewalk double-dutching, when I saw him – a little African-American boy, two or three years old, cute as a button, playing outside in his diaper. I needed to look no further. He would make the perfect little brother.

I slipped away from my double-dutching friends, on a mission. I picked up the little boy, carried him inside my grandmother's house, and sat him in front of the TV. I thought to myself that he needed some toys to play with, so I went back outside to find some sticks and rocks, which, in my opinion, were sufficient to amount to big fun.

When I went back inside to give him his toys, he was nowhere to be found. I ran to my Mom and Dad, frantic, asking, "Where's my little brother?" I explained that I'd just left him to watch TV while I went to find some toys. My Dad thought it would be amusing to pretend that no one had any idea what I was talking about.

I insisted, "I had a brother! I left him right here!" My Dad – finally lit up and said, "Oh, *that* little boy? We gave him back!" I was upset! But… the little boys' mother was more than that.

Apparently, the little boy's mother had been in a panic looking for her child, and upon speaking with my parents, pieced the whole confusing scenario together. My parents, of course, promptly returned her son to his rightful home.

Eventually – granted, a few years later – I did get my wish. My parents had children together, and gave me the siblings I had demanded – another sister and, a couple of years after that, a brother, both, whom I adore.

Even back then, when I wanted something, I wanted it then and there. It was true then, and it's true now: to tell me to stand idly by is to issue an order in vain. I never understand or accept a "no" in any form.

Chapter 5:

Eye of the Tiger

Chapter 5: Eye of the Tiger

Near the end of 6th grade, my history teacher inspired me to take a stand to make a change. This led to me challenging the 8th graders and going head-to-head with our school's biggest bully.

The teacher somewhat reminded me of the actor Richard Dreyfus, although he did have a reddish-brown, wavy hairdo and a small build, no taller than about 5'8. He was so passionate when he spoke about any topic that he sometimes seemed like a tyrant. One day in class, he was speaking about taking a stand to fight injustice and making changes in the world through actions such as breaking tradition, getting petitions signed, and so on.

His lesson mainly moved me because I felt like my entire 6th grade class was facing a major injustice of our own, just because of some silly tradition. Only the 7th and 8th graders were allowed to attend the monthly "Fun Nights" hosted by our school's teachers, and I wanted to know why we 6th graders couldn't go too! Was there any good reason that we couldn't come mingle and play sports and board games and enjoy cookies, cakes, chips, and Kool-Aid with the older kids? I thought not.

As always, I couldn't stand hearing "No," when I asked if we could be allowed to participate. So as I sat in class absorbing all this talk of change and injustice and taking action, I felt inspired not to let this injustice go on any longer.

That day, I drew up a petition for all of the 6th graders to sign requesting permission to attend future Fun Night events, and I worked hard to get the signature of every single 6th grade student on that form. I even convinced some of the 7th and 8th graders to sign it in a show of support. I was on a roll, and news was spreading fast that I was taking on this mission. It looked like I might even succeed.

One 8th grade girl had a major problem with the progress I was making, so she took a stand of her own – not only a stand to fight for 7th and 8th graders to have the right to their own event without us "little 6th graders" getting involved, but also a stand to kick my meddling ass!

This was one huge girl I'm talking about. Not only was she an 8th grader and therefore older than me, but she was taller and 5 times bigger! Word spread fast that she wanted to kill me, but I didn't let it stop me. I just kept on collecting my signatures.

Before I was able to deliver my fully signed petition to the principal, the girl stopped me at my locker, demanding, "meet me here after school tomorrow." It was clear to me that this was an invitation for me to get beat up. She made it clear to me that I could avoid the whole confrontation if I just didn't turn in my petition. It was crystal clear that she was not going to accept having any 6th graders attend her Fun Nights.

I got the message. I didn't turn in the petition... yet. I was a little bit afraid to find out what would happen next if I did, but I had come so far!

That entire night, I was dreading going to school the next day. I couldn't decide what to do. I don't know exactly what came over me, but I turned on my record player and started blasting "Eye of the Tiger," getting myself pumped up, working out in my bedroom, saying to myself, "If this 8th grader is going to beat me up and I am going to die tomorrow, I'm going in with the eye of the tiger. I'm going to fight back."

The next day dragged by. It seemed like the longest day ever. The rumors about how I was going to die were spreading like weeds all over the school. All day long, in the hallways, in-between classes, if kids weren't snickering and whispering about what was going to happen to me after school, they were giving me looks of sympathy as if it was already time to express condolences.

Before the last class of the day, I decided I'd had enough. I had been quivering with fear the entire day, but suddenly I felt something else come over me. I was not going to take this. I was going to stand up for us 6th graders to enjoy the same right to Fun Night as the older kids! I went to the principal, and I handed him my petition.

I told everyone who looked at me with those amused or sympathetic stares that I was ready to fight if that's what I had to do. I had the theme to *Rocky* playing in my head, and I was ready to go and tell that 8th grader the same thing. I was ready for her.

The bell rang and it felt like everyone rushed to the lockers so they could get a good spot and not miss a single second of the big fight. I arrived at my locker first, ready and waiting. My heart was pounding so hard that I thought it'd pop out of my chest – but I was ready to swing.

Then I saw her coming down the hallway toward my locker, where I stood. I thought to myself, "This is my last chance to run," but I let her walk right up to me. And then she stuck out her hand and simply said, "I admire you. Congratulations." Then she shook my hand and walked away.

It was not at all what I expected. I stood there gaping, and I think everyone around was just as shocked as I was. My nerves went from sky high to a flat line. I had no idea what had just happened. I hadn't been beaten up? Why? I had no idea. Was she afraid of me? Did she have a change of heart? Who knows? Regardless, I felt a victory.

The only thing I knew was that I had won. We 6th graders were granted permission to attend all future Fun Nights. I had changed the tradition for not just that year, but for all the years that followed. That day was not a day to be a sissy, and boy, had it paid off!

I think back now about how silly and hilarious that situation was, but it still just goes to show that even back then I was unstoppable, a rebel, and not one to take "no" for an answer – not even when I was shaking in my boots!

From that moment, I promised myself to always have the eye of the tiger.

Chapter 6:

Fruit of My Loom

Chapter 6: Fruit of My Loom

When I was thirteen, I needed money to go to Friar Tucks, the spot where all the kids hung out and played video games. I had Pac-Man fever, and I needed to beat the top score and win all the cool prizes that came with that honor! My parents gave me an allowance, but it didn't begin to cover my game habit.

I quickly learned that in order to raise the kind of money I needed to feed the Pac-Man machine, I needed a better plan than the likes of a paper route. I had gotten tired of trying to collect money and deliver papers on cold Chicago days in exchange for a minimal return on my efforts.

One day, when I noticed someone taking out their garbage, I devised a plan to cash in on taking care of that icky chore for as many neighbors as would let me. I knocked on every door of every floor in the apartments in my area and took out garbage for 25 cents per bag. When every bag I carried down equaled a game of Pac Man I could play, I felt like I was making big money.

It turned out to be an even more brilliant business scheme than I'd imagined since no one wanted to walk up and down flights of stairs just to throw out a bag of garbage. Once I caught on to the real value of my service, I doubled my price to 50 cents per bag. This went on for about a year, until I had finally won the big prize at Friar Tucks.

Soon afterward, my parents moved us out of our apartments and into a house, which brought an end to my little hustle. By that time, I found myself in high school, more interested in fitness, sports and boys than in Fun Nights and arcade games.

My new mission was to find some way to make enough money to buy a car, and 50 cents per garbage bag wouldn't have begun to cut the mustard anyway. The little bit of money I earned in the babysitting and telemarketing jobs I took on wasn't enough to impress me either.

I started getting more creative with my money-making schemes. An older friend of mine worked at fitness health club, so I eventually decided to try my shot at becoming an aerobics instructor. This was during that whole "no pain, no gain" perfect body era, and I loved fitness and needed money – the pursuit made perfect sense to me.

I was much younger than what they had in mind for the person who would be filling their opening, but I went in and convinced them that I'd be perfect for helping them bring in the younger demographic they wanted to target. Yet again, I was not taking no for an answer. I didn't stop selling them on hiring me until I got the "yes" I needed to hear to become the youngest aerobics instructor they'd ever hired. I ended up working there throughout my high school days.

Next, I discovered that participating in pageants and modeling were great new ways to earn extra money, but there was one particular turn of events during my senior year of high school that knocked me down a peg and almost got me into a lot of trouble.

My agency had contacted me in need of female models for a loungewear fashion show. I accepted the offer and arrived at the location to find that not only was this fashion show at a bar full of nothing but men, but also that the organizer's idea of "loungewear" was a wardrobe of teddies and G-strings.

I didn't like the looks of this little scheme they'd arranged. I had no desire to stick around, but I had no cab fare, and the girl who'd given me a ride there wanted to stay and participate.

I was pretty scared of what all of this could look like or, even worse, turn into. The way I was raised had instilled in me the sheer understanding that I was not supposed to be there, or any place, where I was expected to prance around in panties! But I kept my composure and just made the most of my time there by keeping things organized backstage and helping the others get "dressed".

The money the girls earned was a 50 percent commission on each nightie they sold. The pieces were priced at over $150, and one girl sold around 30 in just 2 hours. I was decent enough at math to comprehend that was some good cash for only two hours of work. Still, I just wasn't about to walk around onstage in see-through panties, letting a room full of men gawk at me under the guise of a "fashion show" just to earn a few extra bucks. Yes, I needed the money to buy a car, I told myself, but I couldn't earn it that way.

I don't condemn the women who participated. I learned a lot from that day, between my personal observations and the stories of the other women's lives about the choices they had made and why.

It was like my father always told me: The choices we make in this life are all about what we can handle. What works for one of us won't necessarily work for someone else. That day, I learned a lot about myself and what I could handle – what would and wouldn't work for me. No amount of money was worth that feeling of degradation that I knew I would have felt.

I made it home safely, reflected on my night, and decided to find a new agent who would better represent me.

While it possibly took a little longer than it might have otherwise, I finally earned enough to buy my first car – a navy blue four door Chevy with a sunroof, cloth seats, and an awesome radio and sound system. It was a boxcar a friend of mine had helped me negotiate a good deal on, but I had worked hard for it and it was mine. I had earned it all by myself, and I was proud of it.

I was always a mover and a shaker. I had to be. I wanted too much, and it was in my blood anyway. Moving and shaking never has had and never will have a thing to do with putting my "money-maker" on display in the process, no matter the size of the check. I resolved long ago that I never wanted the fruits of my labors to taste bittersweet.

Chapter 7:

Screeching Halt

Chapter 7: Screeching Halt

It was literally the first day of summer, the day my life came to a screeching halt – June 21, 1988.

I was having the time of my life, and I was pretty damn sure I was invincible.

I had just graduated from high school. I was totally fit, into nutrition and bodybuilding, and the youngest person ever hired to work at the fitness health club as an aerobic instructor. (I *so* wish I could have that body again!) I had won a beauty pageant, and despite my measly height of 5'5, I had also just signed a modeling and acting contract that would land me on billboards all over Chicago. In a matter of weeks, that would put me on the road to Los Angeles, where the rest of my life was waiting for me.

If defying those odds wasn't enough, I was also dating "The Crush."

I had known "The Crush" since kindergarten. By high school, he had evolved into a full-fledged heartthrob – and I was not at all shy about making my affections for my first crush perfectly clear. In sixth grade, I had sent him a secret admirer cassette that played Lionel Richie's *Hello* over and over and over again. For years, my puppy love had only amounted to a close semi-platonic friendship. I still had to give in to the occasional urge to send him a mushy letter: "Will you go out with me – yes or no?" Finally, senior year, I got my "yes."

His mother wanted him to be with someone else. In her eyes, I was a "bad girl" from the other side of the tracks who wouldn't fit in well with the mink-wearing women of her upper class family. In reality, "bad girl" simply meant that I lacked the status of the kind of woman she wanted her son to marry someday.

I suppose she meant well, to put it kindly and give her the benefit of the doubt. She was probably just afraid that her son would fall in love too quickly and get married too soon like she did and then get taken for his money by a girl like me, which was all she had assumed I was about. But we had our own good intentions, and we fell in love – or whatever you call it at that age. So, in the spirit of teenage rebellion, he ignored her warnings against me.

We had gone to the beach, that first day of summer, and then decided to go for a ride on his motorcycle later that evening. Reveling in my perfect tan, my perfect guy and our perfect day, I climbed behind him onto the seat and gripped him tight, feeling free, the wind against me – going Mach speed, we stopped and had a large drink and fries at McDonalds, then at Mach speed we flew past a miniature golf course, then a few eerily quiet residences.

Only a few blocks from my house at just around 10pm, as we drove on Burnham Avenue – which was usually a high-traffic street – my feeling changed to a gnawing uneasiness in the pit of my stomach. I looked around us – no cars in sight.

I couldn't have explained it then, and I can't really explain it now – it just felt like *something* was going to happen. The air around us was suddenly so thick. Maybe it was the hot weather, maybe it was my mood… maybe it was the uncanny observation that there it was, the first day of summer, yet, there was no traffic or people or signs of life anywhere. Something was wrong. Something was going to happen. I could feel it.

I heard "The Crush" scream, "Holy shit!" At that moment, I knew that my senses had been dead on.

I remember feeling calm, relaxed… shutting my eyes and thinking, *Please, God, let me live.* In an instant, I was flying on my back through the air as if on a magic carpet. It felt strange, like I was moving in slow motion. But when I opened my eyes, I saw concrete flying toward my face.

Survival instincts kicked in and my arms flew up for my elbows to hit the pavement instead. I bounced and skidded across the concrete on my right side – then scrambled to my feet and ran down the middle of Burnham Avenue, toward "The Crush."

There had been a car. I had seen that much – a Dodge '88 with headlights that flipped up. "The Crush" was tilted on his side now, facing the car. The bike had flown away from him, and his head was just inches away from the car but, from my angle, it looked like his head was beneath the car.

I leapt up from the ground because my instinct was to run to him and try to pull him from underneath. But he was running toward me already, and instead of screaming in agony like I expected him to, he only pleaded to me in warning: "Don't look at your leg."

I didn't feel a thing – adrenaline, I guess – but you know what happens when someone tells you not to look at something. I looked down. My leg was three times its normal size, and I could see my knee bone protruding from my skin, surrounded by muck that looked like an unsavory mixture of cottage cheese and ketchup.

As the ambulance arrived and the paramedics lifted me onto a stretcher, I noticed a young man about 5'6 tall standing next to a young woman, who looked to be in her mid-20's, crying. I didn't recognize him, but I knew he had to be the guy who'd hit us. I wanted to stand to walk over to place my hand on his shoulder to tell him not to cry to tell him that it was okay... that we were okay.

He had made one of those "Hollywood stops" – paused a little at the stop sign, hadn't seen us coming, sped up, and kept going right through. My knee had gotten caught in one of his headlights. I was wearing a cut-off t-shirt, cut-off sweat shorts, a pair of white Keds – and no helmet. I counted my blessings, for sure.

The paramedics happened to be members at the health club where I worked. Recognizing me, they assured me that I'd be doing aerobics again in no time. As they washed off my leg, I felt refreshed, believing them in those moments when they said I would be okay.

At the hospital, "The Crush" and I were separated by a curtain, so we couldn't see each other. But we talked back and forth constantly through the partition, trying to convince one another that we were all right.

My father rushed from work immediately to come and see about me. By the time my mother arrived and placed her hand on my forehead, I knew that I would be fine. "The Crush's" mother arrived and created a scene, concerned more about whether I might sue them than about how we were feeling.

Meanwhile, the nurses were getting coffee for the doctor to help him wake up for the night shift, a scene that still sticks out in my memory as strange to this very day. Never again in life do I want a sleepy doctor to work on me during an emergency, but at that time I had no choice but put my trust in this one and listen to what he had to say.

I listened as a doctor explained that the gash from the headlight was only centimeters from a main artery in my leg. He told me that most bodies would not be able to heal from injuries like those I had sustained but that, because I was into fitness and bodybuilding, my body was like cardboard, unlike most bodies which were more like paper. Since cardboard is harder to cut through, that major artery had been spared. Once again, I counted my blessings.

A greater sense of relief came over me as I felt the doctors sewing up my leg. It felt like it took forever, like time had stopped – but strangely, I still didn't feel like anything was really wrong with me. Apparently they missed one part of my leg with the numbing shot, because I could feel some of their stitching in an area that didn't seem to be numb. But I didn't say anything. I was in some extreme pain, but all I wanted was for them to get everything repaired so that I could get out of there and go home.

After what I felt like eternity, they seemed to be done stitching, and I asked my mother if they were finished. She told me that they weren't, that they had only sewn the inside. Something like over 280 stitches later – basically half on the inside, half on the outside – the severity began to sink in. I examined the stitches, forming the shape of an enormous "T," and understood that my life had changed.

That was one heck of blow to me, but I refused myself to be a sissy about it. I told myself that I had to overcome it.

I used a walker for the next several months. Continuing to work as an aerobic instructor was out of the question. My acting and modeling contract became non-existent. The move to California was no longer on the agenda. "The Crush" and I seemed to be going downhill, trying to figure out how to make our relationship last.

It seemed that finding my "yes" was not going to be easy at that time. But there's another thing about going through something like that: it shows you what you're made of. That's why - even without my contract, even with the struggles with "The Crush", even with that rather hideous "T" etched into my leg – I was not sure how I was going to make it, but I was going to find my "yes" somehow, in spite of coming to a screeching halt.

Chapter 8:

Cardboard Construction

Chapter 8: Cardboard Construction

Only days before, I had been on top of the world, and now I felt like I had hit rock bottom. My career was over before I'd even had a chance to begin it. I could no longer fulfill my modeling contract. I wouldn't be moving to the West Coast.

I was starting to feel like my flame had completely burned out. Just like my mom a couple decades before me, I'd been stopped in my tracks on that path to California. It seemed like some twisted form of destiny.

The day after the accident was the day I had been scheduled to sign the modeling contracts for my gigs in California. There was no way I was going to make it – not even to the meeting, much less to California. My mother called the agency on my behalf to let them know about the accident that had landed me in the hospital. They couldn't – or probably just wouldn't – reschedule. I had a huge gash in my leg, held together by all those ugly stitches – a modeling career was in no way about to take off at that moment.

Before my accident, I had felt so free and high on life… staying fit… winning pageants… breaking barriers… dating my high school sweetheart… making love on the football field… excitedly taking in everything the world had to offer and looking for even more… living in get-up-and-go-ready-to-rock-and-roll mode. That accident derailed me. It made me shift gears and take a different path leading toward another life, one I had not planned for.

Fitness and pageants had been central in my life, and suddenly I didn't have those to fall back on. I had a lot of healing to do physically, mentally and emotionally. I had to figure out how to keep moving forward in my much more feeble condition after being so accustomed to feeling unbeatable and unstoppable. Besides that, I felt completely undesirable. I kept looking at the hideous "T" shape etched into my leg and feeling like I was in that scene from the movie that Tom Cruise plays a Vietnam solider who lost his legs. I kept thinking, *who was ever going to love me? What was I going to do?*

For days, I just lay in bed trying to will myself to heal. Once I realized it wasn't going to be that simple, I began sinking deep into a mode of self-pity. I received a call from an old high school boyfriend, the head of our varsity football team, on his way to Notre Dame with a football scholarship. He was the biggest guy with the sweetest heart. He told me, "I know you. You can heal from this. Stop feeling sorry for yourself and get your ass out of bed."

This old boyfriend of mine had always been a true leader, and everybody couldn't help but love him. We dated for a little while, but he had ultimately become one of my best friends. He had stood behind me when I made waves by becoming the first "girl" on the varsity football team. I was hell-bent on getting to the bottom of whatever the big problem was with letting me - or any girl - on the varsity team, and he had backed me up. He was the one who had insisted to the coach, "Let her do it." They didn't allow me to play, but I did receive a team jersey and I became the first female manager/ water girl for our varsity football team, paving the way for other girls to have the same opportunity in future seasons.

I had never been the girly-girl type, but always one of the guys – so he forced me to remember who I was and what I was all about in spite of what a sissy I was being right then. I did what he told me to do. I got my butt out of bed and back into the world to kick my healing process into high gear.

Meanwhile, for me and "The Crush," going through something traumatic like that accident together... it's the kind of event that either brings a couple together or rips them apart. In "The Crush's" and my case, it was only a matter of time before it ripped us apart. His parents were primarily the cause of our split.

It wasn't that we didn't try, and I don't think it was really either one of our faults. His parents, then more than ever, made a point of making it as difficult as possible for us to carry on. His father actually did stick up for me sometimes, but I think he saw himself in "The Crush" and that worried him. I think that is what worried his mother as well. They had gotten married right after high school and had children at a young age. I gathered that wasn't what they wanted for their son – the pressure of providing for a family while struggling to maintain a high society image. I never was the type of person that was wanting to get married and have children right after high school - it just was not the plan I had for myself - but "The Crush's" family had plans for him, and I wasn't one of them.

Before the accident, the plan had been for me to attend "The Crush's" college on a volleyball scholarship, but his parents began threatening that, if I went there, they would stop paying his tuition. It felt like the weight of his future was all on me. He told me what they'd said. He knew he could not make the decision for me – it was a choice he'd let me make on my own.

It was a really unfair situation, but faced with making the decision for us, I chose not to accept my scholarship so that he could continue to have his tuition paid. We tried to stay together, but we only lasted on and off for a couple of years. In retrospect, that was probably one of the biggest mistakes I made regarding my education.

Even though I wasn't attending college with him, I made a surprise visit to him once and found a couple of girls in his dorm room. They left when I arrived, and it all seemed innocent enough, but I didn't even have a chance to get too deep into that decision. Before I knew it, we were arguing about something else, which was pretty common for us by that time in our lives. Between his family, the distance, our mutual desires to experience life, our lives charting different paths... plus both of us really did not know what we wanted back then...we finally realized we had no chance to survive, and went our separate ways.

With the money I had won from the pageant before the accident and what my parents gave me along with my savings from working, I was able to put myself through junior college. I worked at a bakery for a while, and then I picked up and started working within financial firms in downtown Chicago, later transferring to Columbia College of the Arts.

I still hadn't given up on my dream of a modeling career and being in the entertainment industry, but a year after the accident, my leg was still in no condition for showcasing to the public. Still, I felt myself bitten again by the bug of no defeat. I was ready to get up and try again. It was time for me to pick up my panties and move on.

First of all, I had to rebuild my leg which was still missing a large chunk of flesh and muscle after the stitches were removed. Over the past year, my body had lost too much fat as a result of the weight loss induced by my meds during my recovery. It took about 10 months for my body to gain enough fat for a doctor to remove some tissue from my rear to fill the gap in my leg and pull the skin tighter, forming a smaller "T". Finally, I was over that hump.

I worked with a talent agency, getting cast as an extra in a few movies, and eventually was discovered by a photographer who invited me to develop a portfolio that he later used to help me into some commercial print.

When another pageant came around, I had to muster up the courage to compete, scar and all. This wasn't the actual official pageant circuit or anything, I saw it as a shot to prove to myself that I was still capable of everything I had achieved once before. There wasn't even a talent competition involved - nearly all judgments were strictly physical: bathing suits, formal wear, pretty appearance, brief interview.

After "The Crush" and I had broken up, I started dating one of the fitness trainers, the "Fitness Guy," one of the guys I knew at the health club who was extremely supportive of my goals and efforts, helping to whip me back into shape. With his help, and my spirit, I felt pretty confident, overall.

Of course, I was the black sheep of the pageant but I was doing it anyway. To me, that was what mattered. I guess I was somewhat of a rebel – I didn't have the boob job, lip jobs, and wax jobs that some of the other girls had. All that I had was the recent repair of my tattered leg and my determination to get back in the saddle. Yet there I was, demanding that they accept my "Well, hell, this is me," approach to the whole ordeal.

The night before the final competition, I went to a Bon Jovi concert, which was obviously a big no-no. I walked into the dressing room running on three hours of sleep, wearing a pair of jeans and a sweatshirt, while everyone else had walked in pageant-ready, all made-up and color-coordinated. I looked like a biker-chick who had mistakenly been plopped down in the pageant world from the wrong side of the tracks. I hadn't even washed my hair the night before. I figured I would just get ready when I got there. They had to be wondering what in the world I was even doing there, but I simply had a point to prove to myself. I was un-rattled by their stares.

"They" didn't matter. I was there to walk across that stage, just like the rest of them, whether they liked it or not.

I knew that I wouldn't win. Given my still very visible scar, I didn't stand half a chance. I was cocky enough to think I might have just a smidgeon of a shot, but that still wasn't the point. I thought to myself, *"Those other girls might beat me, but this scar will never beat me."* It was like getting back on a bike.

I didn't even place. They let us look at the scores and out of roughly 20 contestants, I would have come in something like 10 or 11, from what I recall.

That was my first pageant after the accident, and it wound up being my last pageant altogether. I had proven to myself all that I had needed to: my body hadn't folded like paper, and my spirit wasn't going to either. I was starting to feel a little tougher, as tough as cardboard.

Chapter 9:

It All Started With A Kiss

Chapter 9: It All Started With a Kiss

I had a lot of good times with the "Fitness Guy" I had started seeing from the health club – playing pool on the weekends, going to concerts, hanging out as one of the guys and learning how to put a kit-car together – but between his ex-girlfriend constantly entering the picture and us basically just needing different things than either one of us were able to offer one another, it became apparent that it wasn't going to work out. By the time I met the man I was going to marry, "Fitness Guy" and I were on the verge of calling it quits.

I had no idea during this time, what I wanted to do career-wise, acting and modeling aside. I had just found myself in the financial industry and thought I might stay there. I went after a job at one of the largest commodity firms in the world at the time. First, I met with the secretary, and then HR – and then the man I was going to marry.

When I first walked in, I saw this big hunk of a man – 250 pounds of solid muscle… football player build, just like I liked, stuffed into a business suit. He was powerful, in stature and in status, everything I wanted. My mind wouldn't stop saying, *"Hubba-hubba,"* but I managed to keep my cool in the name of professionalism.

I knew it, though, somehow, the moment I saw him – and in the moment I shook his hand, the deal was sealed.

I don't usually believe in that cliché sort of stuff, but that time it was such a "Mayday!" moment, so much more significant than the butterflies and lightheaded sensations I'd felt in the past when I dated in high school. Prior to "The Crush," I dated the varsity quarterback for a few years and, briefly, a couple of the guys I have known practically my whole life, and just a couple of guys during my early college days. They were all dear to me but I really never felt anything serious enough to take that leap. I just always had my focus set on making my mark in life and I had no time to get really serious with anyone, but this time it was just like in the movies. There may as well have been harps playing in the background – he was "The One," I declared to myself, convinced as I shook his hand, "I don't know what's happening here, but this is the man I'm going to marry."

I'm a dreamer, but reality set in after we spoke and even more so once he offered me the job. He was going to be my boss, and I resolved to go in everyday and look at him as nothing more than that. Frankly, he didn't make that difficult at all. He behaved as my boss in every extreme sense of the word – tyrannical and intimidating, with no discrimination. By the end of my first week on the job, I had revised all those plans I'd dreamt up at first sight. I thought to myself, "No way I'd ever marry this guy."

I became increasingly more convinced of that certainty the more I got to know him outside of our 8-10 hour workdays, through office parties and so on. I couldn't stop wondering what the hell I had been thinking that day at my interview. It all became so hilarious to me. I was 23 years old, I pointed out to myself – he was nine years older than me. So why wasn't he married yet, or at least dating anyone seriously? There had to be a reason. And what was I thinking? Was I really ready at 23 years old?

When I saw the kind of women he dated, I figured I'd found my answer. He fancied himself some kind of ladies' man, but whenever I encountered any of his conquests in the office or on the phones, I found myself less and less impressed with his taste. Working for him, I was always answering the phone and dealing with the girls that called for him. The other girls in the office and I were always joking about his preference for bimbos, a fact which required no exaggeration.

I had been working there for a few months when everyone from the office was invited to go out to a wedding in Wisconsin for one of the other girls who worked there. It was February, and Chicago had just been hit by one of the worst blizzards I'd ever seen, but we were all planning to make the two hour drive anyway. I wasn't about to take on the trip alone in that weather, so my boss told me I could ride with him.

I was heading down the expressway in the snow, coming from where I lived on the South side of Chicago to where my boss lived in the West suburbs, when a truck cut me off and sent my car spinning across the lanes. After doing a full 360, I wound up in the far right lane, on the shoulder of the freeway, thinking once again, "God, please let me live."

I took a deep breath, and then a moment to examine and compose myself. Everything was intact. I pulled my car back onto the road and continued driving – carefully – until I arrived at my boss' home. I was fine, but I remember wondering if I was crazy to just keep on driving after that.

Once I made it to his house, I thought we were just going to head right out and hit the road, but when I got there he offered me a pop (you know, as in what northerners call a cola), showed me around his home, and showed me pictures of his family. I felt a familiarity, a comfort, which I thought it was really nice but also a bit strange.

When we did pack our things into his car to make our way to Wisconsin, I was still in the process of getting dolled up so I painted my nails in the car. He held the bottle of nail polish steady for me while he was driving and I thought that was sweet. From start to finish, a teddy bear - not a tyrant - escorted me on that trip.

We arrived late and still needed to change into our formal wear. I went to my hotel room to put on my dress and he headed to his room to put on his suit, telling me he'd come back and get me so we could go to the reception together. I couldn't zip my dress all the way, so I tried a coat hanger. That didn't work. When he came back, I asked him to zip my dress for me, which became just another sweet, simple gesture that showed me a more softer side within him that I was getting to know.

Since we were so late and the seating arrangement was a kind of a first-come-first-sit sort of deal, we wound up sitting together away from the rest of the people from our office. As everyone gushed over the newlyweds, we chatted it up about what our own dream weddings would be like.

I wanted a true fairy tale wedding – huge, with all my friends and family, a full sit down meal, and a full princess gown… a two-in-one dress that I could remove the tulle from after the ceremony and pictures, to reveal a mini-dress for the reception. He wanted a full-blown top dollar affair with an open bar the whole time – no skimping on the food or drink selection, so that no one missed out on a thing.

At the reception, the band got around to playing a slow song, *Unchained Melody* by the Righteous Brothers. My boss asked me if I wanted to dance, so I joined him on the floor. As the song came to an end, he dipped me. As I came up, he planted a kiss. There that feeling was again. I would never again see him as just my boss.

In that moment, it all started… with a kiss.

Toward the end of the night, when everyone else was heading back to their rooms, my boss and I hung out by the inside pool. We sat there talking for about an hour, and then suddenly, we were making out like we were teenagers. We even prompted a pretty embarrassing, *"Get a room!"* from someone walking by, so I told him that maybe we should go back to one of ours. I wasn't necessarily offering for anything to happen, but thinking back, I have to say to myself, *"What a little slut I was!"*

We were both kind of tipsy. Since I hardly ever drink, a mere two glasses of wine had made me silly. We went to my room, and we talked, and we laughed… and then things just… happened.

We made love, but before we did, he first took a moment to stop me and say, *"Promise me you'll make love to me tomorrow morning."* I had never had anyone say anything like that to me in such a way – so earnest, and so tender, and so vulnerable. If I hadn't been smitten before, I was smitten for sure right then.

So we made love that night… and we made love again in the morning… and we drove back to Chicago, in agreement that we would keep everything under wraps.

As we spent more time getting to know one another better, I was always keenly aware of how strange it felt that, with him, I could be myself completely. It seemed as though I should have found him intimidating – he was such a big, strong, macho man, with these big muscles and this big vice-president title - but for some reason, it felt just right. I liked that he was a big man – it made me feel secure, knowing that he could take care of me in any possible way if ever I did need him to.

After we decided we were serious enough to "go public" and his friends finally met me, their first assumption was that I was just another bimbo he was dating. Like I said, I had seen the types he'd dated before, bimbos from inside out and from top to bottom – extremely young, extremely simple, and ultimately in search of someone to take care of them and the children they'd had by other men.

When his friends sat down and spoke with me, from what I was later told, they had no choice but to come to a different conclusion about me since I neither acted nor spoke like a bimbo. I did begin to understand what drew him to those types of women – he was smarter, more ambitious, more successful, and ultimately in a position (he felt) to control them. He was a typical body-building, egotistical, charming, powerful alpha male – always keeping his "big man" persona intact. But I wasn't his typical yes-girl type – I had determination, I spoke what was on my mind, I had a brain, and I had no problem with fighting back.

Sure, he could be a monster when he was angry, but I had already learned that he was really just a big teddy bear underneath that exterior. There was no turning back once I discovered that side of him. I became fully convinced that the rest was all for show – just him doing what a "big man" has to do to run compliance. I could see right through his act.

He was accustomed to taking people out to very nice, extravagant places but I was so much simpler than all that. I was always suggesting that we just kick back, order pizza and watch movies because that's the kind of girl I really was at heart. One of our favorite movies was *Groundhog Day* – we watched it so much that *I Got You Babe*, the song that played every morning with Bill Murray's character woke up, became one of "our songs". He would cook sometimes, basic things like rice and beans or spaghetti, but it was the thought that counted, and I loved him for it.

When we did go out, it'd usually be somewhere like the arcade to play Galaga and Pac-Man (because I still loved my games!), and then off to play some miniature golf (because that was his sport game of choice). He would always dance in the car while we were on the road, which was a hoot because he had no moves whatsoever – just your typical white boy with zero rhythm – but he did it just to make me laugh.

Every now and then, he would take me on nifty vacations to places like Disneyland, acting like a big kid with me, or to European spas for some pampered R&R, or to a bed & breakfast in Wisconsin just to get away. I still remember playing some lovey-dovey role-playing games at one of the bed & breakfasts. He drew a card that said something like, *"Pretend you just met your significant other for the first time, and act out how you would approach her."* He, all of 250 pounds of him, made the best attempt at a suave Travolta approach that he could manage, walking across the room to plant a kiss on my lips, and we had the laugh of our lives.

There was only one time after our co-worker's reception that I ever got drunk with him, and that was on a cruise we took together from Miami. I remember sitting back and baking in the sun while sipping on piña coladas with our friends. Since I rarely drink, my tolerance level is pathetic – so after all that, combined with two glasses of wine at dinner, it was all over for me. Still, I was still determined to go back out to Captain's Night and wear the sexy dress I had bought for the trip. A wild, random night ensued, somewhere in the midst of which I ordered 16 BLTs from room service, eating 8 of them by myself. Our friends ate the rest while he passed out naked in our cabin alone. When we woke up the next morning and joined our friends again for breakfast, I really had no desire to eat anything but somehow I was the only one who felt great. Everyone else had a hangover. I guess all my BLT sandwiches had done the trick for me.

And at the end of it all, it was one of the best vacations and one of the most hilarious times we had together.

That was the man I got to know and fall in love with. I imagined that we would always be as fun and free as we were during those days.

In those early days, he went out of his way - always - to let me know that I was special, from the littlest to the biggest of gestures. He knew I was the world's biggest Jon Bon Jovi fan, so he would always spoil me with front row seats at his concerts.

Another memory that always stands out to me is of one cold, rainy night after an office party just before wintertime. We were waiting outside for a taxi to drive us to our parking garage. There was a puddle of water between the curb and the cab – so he picked me up and placed me inside before climbing in beside me. When we got to the parking garage, he walked me to my car, dipped me and kissed me before ensuring that I made it safely inside the car and out of the garage.

My gut had known my destiny all along. Who was I to ever question it? When it says, "Yes," I, like anyone else, have to give in to its insatiable demands. I remember watching him in the rearview mirror and thinking, again, that familiar thought to myself, with more certainty this time... that this was definitely the man I was going to marry. And it really all started with a kiss.

Chapter 10:

Enough For The Both of Us

Chapter 10: Enough for the Both of Us

It was just before 6:00 p.m. in the middle of winter and we were running late on our way to celebrate our friends' 11th wedding anniversary. We were driving through downtown Chicago, nearly at our destination, but stuck in traffic on Michigan Avenue.

I asked him if I could have a piece of gum, and he told me to grab it from inside his suit coat. I grabbed his coat from the backseat of the car and fished around in his pockets for the gum. When I popped the gum in my mouth, he smiled, asking, "Didn't you feel something else in there?"

I'd felt something like a box, and asked if that was it – he said it was, and told me to grab it for him. I took it out and handed it over, but he said, *"Open it."* As I did, he asked, *"Will you marry me?"*

I was so shocked that I don't even remember seeing a ring inside the box. I didn't care about the ring. I only cared about what was happening. I said, *"Yes,"* trying to hold back tears, but they started streaming anyway. He asked, *"Are you gonna put it on?"*

I was still absorbing the moment, there on Michigan Avenue. I don't even think everything hit me until we arrived at the Drake Hotel to meet our friends – who had already been in on the fact that tonight would be the night – and I kissed him… Only then did I notice that there was a ring on my finger, just under 3 karats, the biggest, clearest diamond I had ever seen. It felt like a fairy tale.

I learned later that he'd had all of these things set up – we would take a carriage ride and then he would propose to me while we were on Michigan Avenue and then he would kiss me. When we got stuck in our car in traffic on Michigan Avenue, he just went with it. And that made the moment no less magical.

I called my mom and dad and my best friend to tell them the news from the pay phone at the hotel. I was in la-la land for the rest of the night, the happiest woman in the world.

The next morning, I woke up and there was the ring still on my hand. It hadn't been fiction and it hadn't been a dream.

What really sealed the deal for me and determined beyond the shadow of a doubt that this was, indeed, the man I was destined to marry was the day he first met my grandfather – the man who had been my whole world. My grandfather pulled out a photo album and started showing him our family pictures and telling him all our family stories. So there it was: he liked him. It was meant to be.

When my grandfather confirmed, after that first encounter, that he believed this man was "The One," I knew everything would be okay… because yes, in spite of all our great times, in spite of all my butterflies, and in spite of all my internal whispers suggesting the certainty of our future together – there were times when I did have to stop to wonder.

I had always felt so comfortable with myself and I had always been such a cuddly, passionate person. I felt like it was hard for him to ever let go completely and love me fully, with no inhibitions, when it came to intimacy. Being constantly in control of himself and so many others, he was used to defaulting to what I called his "God complex" that he didn't know when to turn it off. I would taunt him sometimes and say, "Big Man, hey Big Man," and he hated that. But

I did it to push his buttons, and I'd remind him, "You don't have to be Big Man with me. I know who you are."

Sometimes, it was what kept the fire going. He would try to control me and I was hell-bent on not being controlled, so in some ways the power struggle became like foreplay. Coming from a loud, passionate family that was always yelling, his occasional fury was normal to me, no big deal. But when he was really mad, he could cut me with his words. He'd catch himself at rest for too long in teddy-bear mode, and it'd suddenly be too much for him – he'd snap Mr. Big Man back to attention and start acting like he needed to remind himself, "Okay, I'm not a sissy."

We would call one another "My Honey" and even had it engraved into our wedding bands. He would say to me, in those days before we were married, "Promise me one thing… promise me that we will always get each other Valentine's Day cards and anniversary presents… something. Let's always remind each other how much we mean to one another, how much we love one another." In practice, he seemed so much different than that but it was still something that he longed for.

It took me a long time to understand. I felt that there was a part of him that hurt – always had – and he didn't know how to stop it.

I felt that it came from his childhood. I remember him telling me a story about how, growing up, he'd receive a swift kick in the balls as prompt punishment for disrupting his mother on the telephone. His stepfather's brand of punishment was to make him sit in a corner for days. Anything happy was consistently taken away from him. When his father bought him and his brother a dog, his mother disapproved and got rid of it just as fast as it had come. Even though he loved fishing and ogled his stepfather's tackle box, his stepfather never once let him touch his equipment or share in that experience that he longed for.

He had all these little stories that amounted to a lot of hurt, all carelessly stuffed behind a fortress. How else could he be? Who else could he have become? How could he know how to love or how to give in to love when he had never been shown that it didn't have to leave scars?

I found out that he hadn't really spoken to his brother for over twenty years, or to his father in just about as long. There was simply no trace of love between them, or none that any of them could detect. It baffled me completely. There I was, rooted within the bonds of my own close loving family - I mean we had some dysfunction like other families but we believed nothing in the world was more important than the strength of ties among kin — but here I was about to marry this man who found such bonds to be completely foreign.

My mom had always shown me lots of affection, and when I needed him, my dad was always there. My family was not perfect by any means, but we knew love. "The One" hadn't had those things. He didn't truly know how to give those things. He didn't understand what it meant to completely show another person that he loved them.

To this day, my mother still warms my sheets, tucks me in, and kisses me goodnight like I'm five years old when I pay her a visit, yet I don't think this man had ever felt that kind of affection a single instant in his life. I didn't mind showing him. I didn't mind being patient with him.

I knew that every family had its trials and that everything was not always peachy for anyone, but I also knew every family's goal was supposed to be to make everything better for the next generation, and then even better for the next. That's what I was taught, and yet I never saw any trace of such an effort among his family. They were good at playing the part, painting a convincing enough picture in public for people to believe that they were a happy, loving family with perfect lives, but it wasn't anywhere near their reality.

From what I understand, growing up, he never really heard his mom say she loved him. When he told me that, it seemed like the answer to everything – or at least the key to understanding everything. That's when I said to myself, within my soul, that I wasn't giving up on him – that I had enough love in me for the both of us, to show him all the love he had never known.

Once I was could understand where all his anguish was coming from, I tried not to let it bother me. I saw through the image of the Big Man to a little boy crying for attention, and I was determined to show him that there was a better life.

He was a man who desperately needed a change. He was full of so much angst and antipathy because of all he had endured as a child in a family of folks who never exchanged hugs, kisses, or "I love you's", spoken or unspoken. Someone had to show him another way… a way of love, compassion, and affection.

I would help us both to find our "yes". I truly believed I had it in me – enough love for the both of us.

Chapter 11:

Monster-In-Law

Chapter 11: Monster-in-Law

The bumps in our road to matrimony came early.

I did not know I was about to be faced with challenges with my hubby-to-be's mother. I felt like she wore that old charming southern smile like a pro, but I quickly got the feeling that she would stab someone in the back like you wouldn't believe. To me, it seemed like she took full advantage of any and every chance she got to say something to hurt us, to drive a wedge between us. She gave me hell since day one, long before we jumped the broom, playing little manipulative mind games even in the dating stages.

At first, it would be little innocent things, like making snide comments about the age difference. If he pointed out Bon Jovi for me on the television, she would say, *"Now, see? I don't know how it's going to last between you two."* And he'd just say, *"Hey! I like Bon Jovi,"* even though he really didn't like Bon Jovi much at all. He was just sticking up for me.

It felt like she was always in our business. She'd given him such a hard time, getting inside his head whenever we had an argument, telling him, literally, *"Stop being a pussy!"* I also recall her, too often, telling him that I was only after his money.

The more serious we became, the more deliberate she became in her actions. After we had moved in together, she would call the house and ask, *"Who is this?"* when I answered, knowing very well who

I was and that I lived there. She was always trying to make worry that there was someone else in the picture, for some reason for me to feel threatened. She would always try to play those sick mind games.

From the day she met me, she decided she liked the girlfriend he'd had in high school better – and constantly reminded me of her preference. She still had a picture up of the daughter-in-law she'd dreamed of (the one she could manipulate) – never, at any point in time that I was together with her son, did she replace her photograph with my own. She thought that she could erase me, and boy was she determined to try anything in her power to make that happen.

A few months after we had moved in together, I decided that I wanted to throw a surprise party for him because he'd never had one before. I invited all his friends, and I invited his parents from out of town to stay with us for the weekend. By this time, we were really getting serious and beginning to talk about marriage, so his mother was becoming increasingly serious about marking her territory.

Upon her arrival, she assumed the role of interior decorator, moving all our furniture and plants around to be the way she thought they should be since, of course, I had done it all wrong. When I put everything back the way it had been, she'd just go and move everything around again. Seriously, she might as well have just pissed all over the floor.

Then, in spite of wanting everything to be just so, she would leave out dirty dishes and do other things like that she wouldn't normally do, just to test me. She was making her list, and checking it thrice: Would I clean up after her? How long would I leave out a dirty dish? Would I call her out over her untidiness? …so on and so on.

One day during that weekend, when he left to go work out, I heard his mother pondering aloud to her husband – deliberately within my hearing range – "What is she going to do when he kicks her out?" She was locked, set and determined to make me believe her son didn't want me. She had no idea that she wasn't dealing with a rookie. I'd been there, done that, and been certified in perseverance. She was no match for the love I felt for her son.

Once she left our house that weekend and went back home, she called him whining and complaining that I had taken up all his time while they were there and she hadn't even gotten the chance to spend any time with her son, so he made a special trip to visit his mom and make it up to her. I even encouraged him to do it so there could be some peace. Throughout his entire visit, I later learned from him, she took advantage of every opportunity to fill his head with lies about me, about all the damage I had done and all the damage I was sure to do – saying that I had been terrible to them while they were visiting and that I was only after his money. His step-father even told him he would disown him if he married me. I mean really??!! It was almost unbelievable.

He may have known that it was all untrue, but he still came back home exasperated. He said to me, *"Marie, out of everyone, you have to get along with my mother."* The mere suggestion that any of this mess was my fault, after everything I'd just had to deal with, was all just too much for me. I responded to him, *"No, she needs to get along with me,"* until I finally gave up and told him, *"You know what? You marry your mother."* And I left – packed my bags and drove off.

I stayed at my cousin's apartment on the west side of Chicago until we worked things out about a week later. Of course, once I moved back in, his mother was up to her old tricks again, asking, *"Which girl is this?"* when I answered the phone trying to plant seeds of suspicion in my mind about what he'd been up to while I was gone. I handed the phone to him, and he wandered into another room, but I could still hear him arguing. At one point, in the conversation he outright said to her, *"No, mother, Marie is not the problem – you're the problem."* Finally, he had put his foot down and gone to bat for me, and it was all I had needed to hear. We had dinner and made love that night, and that was that.

My parents instilled in me as a rule that I am always supposed to respect my elders. His mother made the rule hard to follow. The most respect I could muster for this woman was to get away from her and stay away. He got pretty good at keeping his mother at a distance from me, but I would still hear the occasional petty story about myself through the grapevine, with her at its root. I heard all about how I had to be driven around in limousines and have the finest of everything and have him spoil me and take care of me.

Here's what I found interesting: I had always fought to make my own money. I had my own income, my own accounts, my own car... and yet I was after his money? On what basis? He and his family didn't come from wealth, but it was his mother who was always asking him for money. He always took care of her financially, especially after she got a divorce and so, to her, I posed a threat to her resources and sense of security. All that she could see was that having me in the picture could mean less money for her own pockets, money that she felt she had a right to. She had expected to have my life, to have all his focus, time and attention. Suddenly, she favored him as her oldest and her supporter, after years of depriving him of happiness and of love – and yet, there I was, accused of being after his money.

Of course, his relatives who knew of me only through his mother assumed that every word was true without ever inquiring or getting to fully know me for themselves. With or without any basis in truth, it was a way for them to bond, dogging me out amongst themselves.

But I found out over time that what it really all came down to was the way his family operated. Their misery yearned for company, and they would not tolerate another person's happiness. They all spoke horribly about one another, pitting everyone against each other, and they were much too eager to consume and spread negativity and hearsay. I guess it was just their warped way of welcoming me to the family.

It struck me as profoundly sad, the way they all seemed content to live in the past and wallow in its pain, shielding themselves against any true happiness, and robbing others of their own. What baffled me the most was how any person could endeavor to do everything in her power to destroy her son and crush everything he cherishes, from his dog to the woman he loves. The destructive nature of their dysfunctional interactions driven by such envy and manipulation baffled me completely, although it did help me to better understand the man I loved.

When I eventually met his brother and his brother's girlfriend, I discovered that her story was all too similar to mine when it came to her experiences with that family. She told me all the nightmarish things she had heard about me – the daughter-in-law from hell – but she said that her eyes had opened when we finally met. Once we actually had a chance to experience one another for ourselves, we quickly became friends, bonding over the common wrath we had endured – and monster-in-law didn't like that at all. When she tagged along on vacation one year with us and her sons, she didn't rest until she broke us apart.

I will never understand how, as a mother, anyone could ever rip apart her own children and destroy their families. I would never want to see my children hurt that way. I could never do those things to them and rob them of any hope for happiness. As a mother, an adult, I would never hurt my relationship with my children like that. It makes no sense whatsoever. It was simply insecurity and drama, constantly from the worst monster-in-law, the woman that I had to deal with.

The truth of the matter is that we all have choices. She chose to assign herself the role of the innocent victim, blaming others for her misfortune, and to solicit pity from anyone who would give it to her while she played her family like a deck of cards and robbed everyone around her of the love she herself wanted and needed – from tearing and keeping her sons apart to doing all she could to destroy any of their other relationships as well.

I truly wish I could say something more positive about her, but I suppose I still have some more forgiving to do.

I learned various techniques from some of the marriage counseling we went through and read a lot of books that helped me understand what drove the lies she attached herself to and everything she accused me of – that I was trying to take her son, his money, and the life she felt she deserved – all declarations of the reflection she saw of herself. The truth was, it wasn't me she hated. The real target of her hatred was far more difficult to face.

She is one of the main reasons that I discovered the importance of "The Four Agreements" that Don Miguel Ruiz wrote about – one of which is "Be impeccable with your word", Don't take anything personally," along with, "Don't make assumptions," and "Always do your best."

My word? I have vowed to myself to live my life in a way that enables me to look in any mirror and be happy with the person I see.

My monster-in-law, along with the lessons ahead that I would learn from my husband, showed me that in everyone, in everything, there is a lesson to be learned. Facing my demons and struggling to understand the goblins in my midst are the only way to find my "yes" through any obstacle. If nothing else, they have taught me what and how *not* to be. That's why I'm not afraid of the Boogeyman, nor am I daunted by any monster-in-law.

Chapter 12:

Wedding Season

Chapter 12: Wedding Season

On the morning of May 30, 1998, monster-in-law gave me pearls, a nice gift and a seemingly kind gesture – until you factor in that she was a divorcée... passing down pearls from her estranged and despised ex-husband... to me, someone for whom she'd never had a kind word... on my wedding day.

Just in case she hadn't protested loudly enough before, that gesture spoke volumes and I heard her message loud and clear. Just in case I missed *that* one, she also mentioned that she wanted one of her friends to sing a song at our ceremony that he'd sang at hers. Needless to say, I did not bother ever finding out how the pearls looked around my neck – and her friend kept that song to himself.

Try as she may, there was nothing she could do to ruin the majesty of our wedding day. Neither her comments to other family members nor her behavior was going to ruin my day, our day.

We had precisely the wedding we had fantasized about, from all my friends and family being there and the full princess gown at an elegant ceremony, to his full-blown top dollar open bar affair with no skimping and all the fixings at our reception. There were nearly 500 guests (483, I think).

Just before the doors opened for my father to walk me down the aisle and give me away, I turned and asked him, *"Any last words for me before handing me over?"* He turned to me and answered, *"**Kid, what**

works for me isn't going to work for you. And it's not all about love. It's about what you can handle." When the doors opened, I looked down the aisle and saw my soon-to-be-husband standing there. The One. I looked at my dad and said, *"I know there will be ups and downs. It'll be a bumpy road, but I can handle it."*

When I heard my groom's speech and watched him standing there declaring in front of everyone how much he loved me, I knew more than ever before that this was exactly where I was supposed to be.

We exchanged our vows and our kisses. (I never did like the "obey" business, by the way — what a scam. What the hell were they thinking? Who says I have to obey?) Finally, the moment arrived and we walked down the aisle as husband and wife.

Outside, a Rolls Royce pulled up to escort us to our reception. On stage at the reception hall was one of the top bands in Chicago, and as they announced our arrival as newlyweds, I felt like a princess, walking with my husband to our seats. We had a roped off tables full of sweets, from one end of the building to the other. There was a five-course meal awaiting us and all of our guests had a rose placed on the back of their chair. The aroma of roses filled the entire room all night long. Everything we planned and organized and decided together was simply a fairytale wedding.

When we got home after the wedding, I had so many bobby pins I could not wait to get out of my hair... but I wanted to get all my thank you cards written before the honeymoon, so my husband sat and removed all my bobby pins for me while I drafted the cards. I have always thought that it was one of the sweetest things....

We took a 23 hour plane ride to get to Fiji for our honeymoon. When we arrived there, we had to then take a private plane over the pure blue waters to Turtle Island where *The Blue Lagoon* had been filmed. The islanders greeted us with a song as we flew in. We went shark fishing, snorkeling, had our own elegant island bungalow. During one of our fishing escapades my husband caught dinner for everyone on the island, as a matter of fact! We drank kava like the natives, and enjoyed top of the line everything in the midst of other prestigious figures and couples.

It was an absolutely perfect week… no cell phone, no work, no family…just us. It really was like Fantasy Island.

I believed in every moment, and I soaked up every second. I had met the man of my dreams… my knight in shining armor had ridden in on the proverbial white horse and swept me off my feet, just like every little girl dreams about. The stuff of fantasies had become my reality, and I was primed to have a fairy tale life.

And so, we lived happily ever after….

Chapter 13:

Happily Ever After, the

Sequel: Honeymoon's Over

Chapter 13: Happily Ever After, the Sequel: Honeymoon's Over

I had met the man of my dreams, my knight in shining armor riding in on the white horse. I thought the fairy tale had become my reality.

All of that now feels like a billion years ago. I was so young... I had no idea.

Yes, like I'd told my dad, I knew there would be ups and downs, and I was ready and willing to overcome them and stay together. I had no idea it would be a roller coaster.

Growing up in a Catholic-Italian-Hispanic and Polish household, divorce was unheard of as an option. Even though my parents were both previously married and divorced, they wanted to make sure I would learn from their mistakes. They knew how to teach me the right way to handle things from their experiences. Like my dad said, *"What works for me is not going to work for you. You live the best way you can, you can't control others and It's not all about love, it is what you can handle."* But what my grandparents (old school ways) taught me was that a husband and a wife worked it out and stuck it out, the "it" that was not working – whatever "it" was - didn't matter.

It seemed like instantly after our actual honeymoon ended the proverbial honeymoon was also over.

Thinking back on it only a week later felt like remembering a good movie… like it was fiction… like it had never been real.

My husband went right back to work – and never seemed to stop.

Meanwhile, he didn't want me to go back to work, saying that he could take care of the finances. I asked him, if I accepted an allowance and stayed home instead of working, whether he would treat me like a peasant and act as lord over me, obsessively asking what I was doing with every penny I spent. He assured me that wasn't what it would be like, but he did not keep that promise.

Giving in to that idea was probably the biggest mistake I ever made. Before my nuptials, I'd had my own paychecks, I'd had my own bank account, I'd had my own checkbook, and I'd called my own shots. Now, my husband controlled the finances and I had an allowance and subordinate access to a joint account. He had designated himself as responsible for all financial duties between us. Period.

I was young and naïve. I had set not a single ground rule for what I needed in my marriage. He was nine years older. I looked up to him in many ways, with all that he'd accomplished in his life beginning at such a young age. I was his number one cheerleader, so I went ahead and let him lead.

I admit it was fun at first. He basically just put a credit card in my hand and turned me loose. Compared to what I was used to, I suddenly felt as if I had unlimited means to buy all the nice things I wanted, from groceries to clothes to furniture, without having to bat an eye about the cost. It felt liberating, but that was an illusion. Nothing is free. Everything costs something, I would learn that in due time. What felt like financial liberation would only amount to its own unforeseen form of bondage.

Meanwhile, I busied myself with the task of making a home. I didn't want to live in the house his mother had decorated for him – I wanted something that was all our own, something fitting as we began our new life together. He gave me a price range, let me loose with a realtor and told me to find three houses that I liked. From those he'd choose the one he liked most. The one he chose was the most grandiose, of course -- and of course, as far as everyone else was concerned, I was the one who'd demanded the biggest and the best of everything.

It was a beautiful home. My closet was the size of a bedroom and the kitchen went on for days. The butler pantry and dining room seemed like it was made for the Roman Empire and I got lost in it, especially when my husband would go overseas for work as frequently as he did. There I was, this simple South-side Chicago girl who really just liked pizza and movies – nothing complicated - and yet nothing around me seemed simple anymore.

I remember that I began feeling alone, isolated... different... and I more or less withdrew from the rest of the world and suddenly it seemed like I didn't fit in anywhere anymore. I was 28 years old - too young for his friends, and no longer able to relate to my own friends who were living drastically different lifestyles than I was living.

I buried myself deeper in home-making duties. I spent all of my time decorating or watching cooking shows and playing chef in the kitchen (even though his diet for the longest time was a mere nine hard-boiled eggs per day and whatever else body builders eat).

Over the years, after my children were born and as my husband climbed the corporate ladder and advanced in his career, he behaved increasingly as though he didn't trust me. I needed his permission for every little thing, every insignificant purchase, every single decision. He, a guy who'd almost failed art class, demanded the right to executive approval on everything, down to bathroom decor decisions, because he simply had to have the upper hand. He would tell me "No," just to feel like he had control – just to remind me that he could, and would, because he was the one in control. It was all because he was losing control of what was going on at work along with what, in his mind, a husband and wife do and the roles they are supposed to play. That is what I later understood, but at that time, I resented it. Each day spent with him was practice for me in finding and demanding my "yes".

It was an ongoing battle over the years, and anytime that we would try to talk about it, I would get screamed at like I was a child. It would then become an argument, so I began to wonder, "why should I even try?" I decided to just let him handle it. Eventually, that was how I came to be controlled.

From not handling a checkbook to having absolutely no say-so in financial planning or finances, my life had become exactly the life I had always sworn that I would never live.

My grandmother had never written checks. My mother had never driven. The men in their lives ruled the nest. Even though I loved my dad and my grandfather dearly, my life was supposed to be different than the ones they had given my mother and grandmother. In my mind, it was supposed to be better. It was suppose to be about me finding someone who would not control me or rule the nest. It was suppose to be – I find someone to allow me to be me and we rule together. The new generation of marriage.

Yet there I was, married to a man with so much control over my do's and don'ts, my can's and cant's, that I couldn't even be the first to open my own mail. He had to intercept it first, commenting that I was like a drug user, and toss out anything he felt I didn't need – magazines, catalogues and so on. Anything that didn't meet his

81

approval, didn't meet my eyes. He deleted Desperate Housewives episodes so that I "wouldn't get any ideas." He managed all of our money because I was, in his opinion, "too irresponsible" to handle finances, and occasionally, he would demand that I make an effort to fit in with the executives' wives and with the school mothers too. I guess he had this image of the "Perfect Housewife" that I was supposed to live up to in order to help paint the image in his world of standards.

I felt like it was all about control, especially with finances. If he went to Vegas and ran up a $30,000 gambling tab, it was well-deserved leisure. If I went to Neiman Marcus and charged $2,000 on a credit card, I was eating our finances alive. The truth was, at no time were we ever hurting for anything. He could do what he wanted, but I needed to answer to him. It was just his way - wanting to control what I spent – to remind me that it was all his.

He really pushed me to "fit in" with other mothers, but I was not your typical mother. Yes, I would do all the typical motherly duties and beyond. Anything but "coffee clutching." Unfortunately, the mothers he wanted me to be around were women who did nothing but gossip about other people and thrive on non-sense and that was not appealing to me. I was only just beginning to be pushed into this world of trophy wives and pure control.

It was an effective mind game, you see. Anytime he "let me" have something, I had to pay for it by hearing all about it later. On the flip side, he often bragged to everyone about how I was the perfect wife and how he gave me everything because he just wanted me to be happy. To everyone I knew, it looked like I was an ungrateful person who had this perfect life, yet, I kept demanding more and more from him because I was never satisfied. He did believe that he gave me everything, but I didn't feel that I had everything. For everything he did give me, there was a hidden price to pay in return. In reality, all that I wanted was his attention, so when I learned what grabbed it, I used it. I really only wanted his love.

The bottom line was, just like for everyone else we were around, it was all about this "image." It was not about any kind of real "love". Because I was searching for that love from him, not concerned with the image or things around me, I learned the best way to get his attention was to charge something on the credit card. Eventually, I learned how to thrive off the negative attention because it was really the only kind of attention I knew how to get from him. I had to hit him where it would hurt him, by spending his money, to get a few minutes of his time and a little of his focus. By the same token, it became his way to avoid giving me that attention that I craved. When he didn't want me in his hair, he would give me money to go spend just so he wouldn't have to deal with me. I fell completely into the game. It was the same game a lot of others around me had been playing for a long time.

Everything always turned into an argument. I didn't know anything, as far as my husband was concerned. I was a dummy who was not to be trusted to handle *anything* because that was his job. My job was to handle the responsibilities of the house and nothing more. If I tried to chime in during a conversation about finances, he would say to me in front of everyone, "Stick to what you know when speaking."

I had come a long way from living in a food stamp household, and now that I had so much, it seemed unreasonable to complain about anything I didn't have. Still, I ached for some autonomy. I needed to begin making decisions for myself and doing some things on my own. I had a brain, I had ambition and I had knowledge. I had passion and love, and I had a purpose and I had the eye of the tiger. I was determined to take on the world with all this burning inside me, I was still here… controlled and disrespected. Thinking back, I realized that I was just being programmed to be something I was not.

I had thought that I was entering into an equal partnership, but as I reflect on that time, I had really become nothing more than a trophy wife. I needed to feel like something more. I needed to shine. I needed to contribute. I needed to feel valuable. I needed to feel loved, honored and respected by my husband.

The reality was...the fairy tale...the honeymoon... was over.

Chapter 14:

Mission Aborted

Chapter 14: Mission Aborted

Eight months after the kiss that started it all, I left my job at the company so that the man I worked for and the man I was surely destined to marry wouldn't be one and the same. I had no idea that, whether I worked for him or not, he would muscle his way back into that position of power eventually, but I digress...

After leaving the company, I had a short stint with another financial firm that I ultimately had to file a sexual harassment case against. That, I suppose, turned out to be another kind of blessing since that led me to eventually work for the man I have come to consider as my mentor and the ultimate rock star, Richard Sandor. The financial firm I worked for prior to working for Richard's firm gave me an experience, one that I really had to wear some tall stilettos to survive. I was one of five women on the OTC trading floor with over 200 men. I was not only sexually harassed by my main boss, but also the target of daily comments made by others that were also very degrading. When I complained to the heads of the firm, people that I thought could protect me, they retaliated by trying to demote me. One of the men went as far as to say it was normal behavior. To make a long story short, after being demoted and then hiring an attorney to sue them for the wrongful behavior and demotion, I later had to go after my attorney who made an underhanded deal with the firm I worked at. The firm offered him a deal to convince me to settle (all of these things I can't legally prove but they did happen under the table). I had to deal with all that on top of dealing with all the snickering and humiliation I encountered. In the end, this all made me realize that I really needed even taller stilettos in the world of business. Being a woman surrounded by the world of men was just not for sissies, indeed!

When I went into the interview for Richard Sandor's company, the vice-president there – a female – saw fit to hire me against Richard's will. I had been completely honest with them, revealing that I was leaving the previous large financial firm I had worked for due to sexual harassment, and that I was about to marry someone from the previous financial firm where I'd been employed before that. At the time, I don't think Richard was comfortable with the number of contacts I had already established in that industry, my controversial history and he wondered where my loyalties would lie... I felt that he wondered whether I would share secrets with my fiancé's firm – things like that. From what I learned much later, the vice-president saw the eye of the tiger in me then and I reminded her of herself. Unlike other men I dealt with previously in the business world, Richard - who comes from a different breed of men, the kind of men that respect women in the industry - decided to let her hire me at her discretion anyway.

When I first started the job, I was cocky. One particular day, I walked by his secretary's desk and she was all tied up with the phones, so she asked me to help her out a little. She asked me, "Hey, can you get him a can of Coke?" I huffed past her, making it perfectly clear what my position was and that she must have lost her mind – I was more of a compliance assistant, definitely not a secretary. After what I had gone through, now that I was sharing an office with the vice-president, I thought that it should have been obvious that fetching cola for thirsty CEO's was beneath my pay grade – or so I thought until the VP confirmed that I did indeed need to fetch him a can of pop as requested.

I was not happy, but I went to get the pop anyway, still huffy as I brought it back to her, when I returned, she was on the phone and hardly even glanced at me, waving me back into his office to give it to him myself. I'm still feeling cocky at this point, and a tad irritated by the degradation of this task, so when I go to place the can on his desk, I'm (foolishly) expecting a thank you... or any form of acknowledgement at all. I got nothing. I had a hard time swallowing that. I was going to make this man see me and address me, so I turned back as I was walking out, and said, "Be careful, I shook that up." As soon as I said it, I thought, *"Oh shit, I'm fired."* I knew that he hadn't really wanted to hire me anyway, but I only heard him laughing behind me as I scurried on out of the door. So I think I succeeded in getting his attention. I must have made him wonder, *"Who in the hell is this little shit?"*

As time went by with me working in the office, Richard had a growing sense that I was a headstrong woman on a mission to get things done. Most people, when they walked past him or stood next to him on the elevator couldn't resist to opening up their mouths to interrupt and say something to him. I was never that person. I wanted to be vice-president someday and I wasn't tolerating any silliness in that office, especially after all the chaos at the last place.

One particular day, I was blazing past him as I usually did on my way to get something done, and I heard him declare, "Now that's what I like, a woman with a purpose." After hearing that, we became friends, and he continued to inspire me every day that I was employed there. If I went in to ask him a question, he would answer it and give me advice. I stopped feeling intimidated by his status as CEO/ Founder of the company. He was so well-known, but still so down to earth. He rarely took limos. He took the train, or he would walk. Everybody liked him. Actually, I wanted to be just like him. He was so smart, and such a true inspiration.

We were a small company during the time I worked there, but at some point, he sold the company and some of the people had to leave. I was one of those people. I could only thank him. There were absolutely no hard feelings. I had learned so much and grown so much from working there with him.

I got married shortly after leaving, but I always kept in touch with him, the secretary and the vice-president from the office. I still went to all the office parties at their new company, and always made it a point to visit when returning to Chicago after I had moved. No matter how much more he did and accomplished in his life, I knew I could go back to him and confide in him what I wanted to do – that I wanted so much to be like him. He was my rock star. He inspired me. I was a woman with a purpose, and he was the one who noticed that.

By now, I had a husband who insisted that if I got a job, I would only cost him more money. A professional status of my own would mean professional clothes that he'd have to buy for me. Pointing out that the money I'd bring in with a salary would more than compensate for the little bit spent on new attire wasn't even worth the effort. It was always to no avail.

I tried working at a part-time job and later starting my own business, but he always complained about my endeavors non-stop. He insisted that not only did I not have to work, but that I shouldn't work – that I should take care of the responsibilities at home.

Marriage should be about holding hands and flying together. That's what I wanted. But he'd said to me, "I don't want to live your life."

Just because he didn't want to live my life, did that mean that I couldn't live it either?

My mission to become a vice president or the CEO of a major firm was basically aborted at that point.

Chapter 15:

Pariah in the Bible Belt

Chapter 15: Pariah in the Bible Belt

One year into our marriage, after losing the job I had with Richard Sandor and then becoming a housewife, a man in Memphis made my husband a job offer he couldn't refuse. So he left the company in Chicago where he'd worked for over a decade, and we picked up our lives to move down South.

Memphis was only about an hour and forty minute flight from Chicago, an 8 or 9 hour drive. I contemplated, how different could it be? It wasn't too shabby for Elvis – who was I to thumb my nose at the city the King of Rock had called home? The more I thought about it – a new city, a change of pace – even though I was a little nervous to be leaving the only place I had ever called home, I was pretty excited for this chance at a fresh start in our life together as one. So I packed up to leave my entire support system of friends and family behind and venture to a place where I knew no one.

From the very first time we met with them, my husband's company wined us and dined us so much that it reminded me of *The Firm*. The way they invaded every aspect of our transition. They took us to dinner, promising us over and over again that we would all be just like family. They insisted on "assigning" us their realtor and "steering" us toward the part of town they wanted us to live in, but I was determined for us to decide that on our own.

Once again, my husband told me to pick out my three favorite homes, saying that he'd make the final decision from among them. I looked at over forty homes and finally narrowed it down to three. Once again, he chose the grandest of the bunch, in a gated community on a golf course, not that I had any complaints.

On moving day, we pulled up to our new home in a long, black Lincoln town car. I stepped out wearing my big hair and a leather jacket, looking like a mafia princess straight out of Chicago's South-side. I peered up and down the block, taking in the preppy-looking neighbors in golf clothes, some with crisp jeans and tees. To say that I stuck out like a sore thumb would be an understatement. I felt like a major disruption to an otherwise flawless *Stepford Wives*-esque kind of set-up, looking more like Marisa Tomei's character in *My Cousin Vinny*.

The day we moved in, I got my first taste of what many people refer to as "southern hospitality." As soon as they caught sight of our moving vans, the neighbors invited themselves over, welcoming us with breads and pies. One neighbor even came in without bothering to knock and wait for an invitation to come inside.

It didn't take long for me to realize that some of my neighbors' penchants for warm welcomes were simply disguises for pervasive nosiness that had no end. One woman waltzed right into my home and started a conversation with one of our painters about "the people" moving in and about the work she needed done in her own home – she didn't even seem to notice me standing in my own dining room. She had actually seen me but mistakenly assumed that I was one of the workers – I guess because my ethnic look and because the notion of wearing a baseball cap and sweats for any other reason was unheard of, bless my heart!

Everywhere that I went, people who noticed my new face would pry, asking the same odd questions. What high school did I go to? (Never what college.) Where does my husband work? (Never where

I work.) What church do I belong to? (Never *whether* I belonged to any church.) Would I like to attend their Bible study? Eventually, I realized that these questions were just their way of sizing me up.

I accepted an invitation to join a new neighbors group, figuring that I would get to know my neighbors better. They'd invited me to a luncheon to discuss fundraising ideas for their organization, so I walked in full of energy, like a bat out of hell, into this room full of older ladies who had also moved to Memphis from other cities, along with many blue-blood women whose gut reactions were to run like hell before I got too close. You'd have thought I was Madonna strutting in wearing her "Material Girl" ensemble.

As a group of much older women – I wasn't even 30 by that time, which made me the youngest person in the group – they felt a constant need to try to put me in my place. The idea behind the invitation, I realized too late, was that they wanted to help me adjust and fit in, so they didn't take too kindly to the idea that I didn't necessarily care to fit in – and they definitely didn't appreciate my own ideas about helping them with anything.

I didn't realize that there was a pecking order, and that I was expected to earn my stripes first. These women had always done things a certain way, and they made it clear that they weren't interested in hearing – much less doing – anything new.

Unfortunately, I was inclined to having great ideas and looking for where we could make good things even better. My attitude was generally that we don't have to necessarily reinvent the wheel – but can't we make it bigger? Adding to a discussion about a bake sale, suggesting that we compile a cookbook, or suggesting the idea for a luncheon could expand into plans for a gala, to them, was all me overstepping boundaries. The entire room would break into an uproar.

Not all of these women were unbearable to handle, but as a unit they struck me as a complacent clique, people who were more or less all the same. My way of dealing with them was to accept who they were and respectfully demand the same in return. Apparently, their way of dealing with me eventually became tuning me out altogether.

At another event they had invited me to, a luncheon at the Orpheum Theater, I greeted everyone as I sat down at the table I'd been assigned, but no one seemed to hear me. I gave them a few moments, and then I tried again. Still nothing. Either someone would interrupt my every attempt to speak up, or someone would follow my statement with a statement completely unrelated to what I'd said.

It occurred to me that maybe they, these southern ladies who were so stereotypically legendary for their hospitality, really and truly could not hear me because they were old. So I spoke up louder, as a last resort, yelling, "CAN ANYBODY HEAR ME?!" They stopped, looked at me... and then carried on with their conversation just as they had before.

I was trying, I really was, but the transition to a southern gal lifestyle was becoming overwhelming. On top of trying to use less profanity and dial down my general Chicago-ness so as not to offend the belles around me, suddenly, I also had to wear fancy gowns out to more and more events where the people who'd invited me behaved like they wanted nothing to do with me once I arrived.

Even shopping became just another opportunity to be shunned. I can't even count the number of times I felt like Julia Roberts in *Pretty Woman* because no one wanted to assist me whenever I entered some upscale store in my baseball cap – until I whipped out my husband's credit card. Still they acted as if I had some plague around me.

When I started exploring the city, doing some sizing up of my own, everything just felt wrong. I went downtown and found that what should have been the liveliest part of the city was actually more like a ghost town. There was no one hanging out, nowhere to shop. Between the scrutiny of my judgmental neighbors and the absence of any signs of life or lovers of it, I started feeling like Kevin Bacon in *Footloose* – a damn Yankee "troublemaker" who'd landed in a country town.

Even something as simple as going to a Chinese restaurant became a trying experience to adjust to – I had never in my life heard Chinese men speak with southern accents. It sometimes worried me that they wouldn't know how to actually make Chinese food.

In Chicago, I had gotten used to walking into a foreign restaurant, whether it was Chinese, Italian or German, and being surrounded by cooks and waiters who were actually from the country of the featured cuisine, having the accent to go with it, or at least speaking the language. Now, no matter where I went here in Memphis, no matter what culture, no matter what theme, all I heard were Southern accents.

I tried to keep my composure, but the final last straw came when I finally broke down and went to an Italian restaurant, seeking the comfort and familiarity of my roots. Everyone I had spoken to claimed this place made the best Italian food in town – but after I tasted the Chicken Marsala I had ordered, I burst into tears. I tasted nothing of my culture. I was used to something else, something so completely different, and it sank in that I would never be able to find it here.

Every day, it became progressively more and undeniably clear that I wasn't in Kansas – er, Chicago – anymore.

In spite of the many obstacles, I was determined to convince myself of the possibility that the wretched "T" etched into my leg from the stitches after the motorcycle accident had been for "Tennessee."

Maybe, just maybe, this place was – somehow – exactly where I belonged. I had to try to make some changes to fit in because, truly, I was the pariah in the bible belt.

Chapter 16:

Born in My Heart

Chapter 16: Born in My Heart

Three months into our marriage, I was ready to begin our family.

Up until that point, I had always been so sure that I would never want children. I was 13 years older than my brother and sister – which meant that, growing up, I was the default babysitter and it drove me nuts. After high school, I was pursuing a modeling and acting career so I only saw having children as an interference against reaching the highest possible levels of celebrity. After the motorcycle accident, I revamped my mission, aiming to become a successful business woman. At every stretch, my mindset had been, "Look out, world – here I come!" so it seemed that the possibility of having children would only slow me down. Heck, even marriage had been a back-burner concept originally.

But then came the uncontrollable feelings that set in as soon as I met the man I knew I was going to marry. My dreams had already become replaced with his dreams and the role of becoming his number one cheerleader. It became a matter of when, not if, I was going to get started on my own tribe of little MVP's. I suddenly just felt… ready.

The extent of my husband's opinion on the matter was that if we had a girl, he wanted to name her Jennifer – that was as far as he had gotten. Just like with me, there had never been anyone or any reason to make him give much thought to the idea of having kids. He'd had no qualms dealing with the children of the women he'd dated in the past, but he had never dwelled much on any thoughts or desires of having his own. After we came together, it just made sense to us both to start trying. It seemed straightforward enough.

After about a year of "trying," it just wasn't happening – and I've never been known for my patience. I needed to know what the heck was wrong, so that we could get moving on making this baby we wanted.

I could remember a check-up when I was 19 years old. When the doctor had warned that I might have "some trouble" once I decided to start trying to have children. I hadn't understood what he was talking about at the time, and I didn't bother to inquire further – like I said, in my younger days, having kids had been the furthest thing from my mind. Aside from that, telling me that I can't do something has never stopped me from thinking that I very well could do it anyway if I damn well pleased – not even biology could tell me what to do.

Still, as I remembered this, I figured that I'd better go see someone for some deeper insight. We both went to visit our doctors, and we were both told that there was absolutely nothing wrong with either one of us. I suspected that the trouble I was having with conception possibly had something to do with my motorcycle accident. The doctor decided to put me on medication to help me ovulate. I set aside my usual hesitation about introducing extraneous chemicals into my body. It seemed worth the risk in this case.

The pills made me loony! Somewhere in between the first pill I popped and a night of crying hysterically while packing bags angrily, threatening to leave my husband simply because he declined a dinner invitation from my mother, it became clear that the side effects were a little too much for me to handle. It was then that I set the pills aside and returned to my doctor, who suggested hormone injections as an alternative.

My husband and I couldn't understand why I should have to go through all of that if there was supposedly nothing wrong with me. We decided that it was time to end all this with the doctors and the chemicals.

I wanted to have children, and if biology wasn't going to be on my side then I would take matters into my own hands. The household I had grown up in with my Dad who was technically, by society's standards, my "stepfather," yet who was every bit as loving towards me as my mother had been – and certainly far more worthy of the "father" title than the man who had merely donated his sperm to the cause – had shown me that people don't have to be linked by blood in order to be a family. We had ups and downs just like any other father and daughter, but our bond grew over the years and was also just as strong. I understood that what mattered was love, not blood.

Once I started doing some serious research into my options, exploring everything from adoption processes to agencies, it seemed like everyone around me made it their business to issue the same irritating warnings. I felt like I was hearing a broken record. I can't count the number of times I heard, "Marie, it could take years before anyone approves you for a domestic adoption – maybe you should adopt from overseas to hurry things along," and "You should just go to China and adopt through their system because it's faster."

None of that made any sense to me. It was not that I had anything against the prospect of adopting from China, but there were too many children right here in America that needed loving homes. I wasn't just going to accept that, in order to bring one into my family, I would have to take my search overseas. I thought to myself, "Well, so be it. I'll just have to wait years and years," but there was no way that a "no" was a possibility in the matter.

I stuck to my guns and told myself, "I don't care how long it took everyone else. It's not gonna take me that long." It's not just that I wouldn't take no for an answer – I simply wasn't going to believe it. Period.

When I came across information about a place in Texas that specialized in adoption, I was immediately drawn to its history and philosophy. Founded by a woman who had taken an indignant stand against the outdated thinking that any child in the world could be regarded as "illegitimate," the institution was dedicated to putting a stop to the custom of stamping the term on the birth certificates of adopted children. She had declared that there were no illegitimate children – only illegitimate parents.

I have always been spiritual and believed in a higher power so I really never worry too much. I prayed about what I wanted and despite all the warnings about the tortuous length and procedures of the approval process to be matched as an adoptive parent, this agency matched us almost immediately. I don't know whether it came down to luck or speaking it into existence, but in any case it came to be. Within three months, we had been matched with a birth mother, and my son was born six months after that. That proved undoubtedly to me that there is a heaven because my prayers were answered.

I fell in love with my son before he was even born. Throughout the months of our birth mother's pregnancy, I spent hours on the phone with her, talking from late at night to early morning hours. I was there for an ultrasound, a few doctor's visits, and the day she gave birth by C-section in the delivery room. I was able to also experience everything the father usually does, and every bit of it was amazing to me.

There is no possible way that any person could understand without experiencing for themselves the gift, the love, the utterly divine experience of what I witnessed and what I lived in those moments and during the months leading up to them. To evolve from a woman, (apparently), physically unable to bear children, into a woman consummating her power to become a mother nevertheless was an experience that I will forever treasure. I have boundless love for the birth mothers to whom I will always be grateful for my son and, later, for my daughter.

I didn't want our son to be the only loved and spoiled kid in the house. Besides, he needed a sibling. I really wanted another child to complete our family. When my husband and I decided again later that we were ready to have another child, we tried again on our own first, but we pretty much knew what to expect – nothing happened. We had no qualms about returning to the adoption agency.

Of course, I had to hear from the skeptics again, those who insisted upon enlightening me that the adoption process is even *more* difficult the second time around because birthmothers will worry that a child that is already in the household will take attention away from the child they would birth. Of course, I ignored the insights and went on about my endeavor as I'd planned.

We were matched with a birth mother just as quickly as we had been matched the first time. Once again, I had the opportunity to build a relationship with the birth mother during her pregnancy and witness the vaginal birth of my daughter this time in the delivery room. All over again, I fell in love, knowing this meant that life had given to me two of its most beautiful blessings.

Our children had definitely brought my husband and me closer, connecting us eternally. I honor my children's birth mothers for the gifts they bestowed upon our lives – but that's between us. Between my family and the rest of the world, they are simply our children. End of story.

I've never liked saying that they're adopted. I've come to loathe the term. I'm not embarrassed by it at all, but I detest that there's any distinction. I feel like it shouldn't even be a factor. The adoption agency had declared there are no illegitimate children, only illegitimate parents. In the same way, these were not my adopted children, only my children. When people apply superfluous terms to us, I feel like they're stamping that same label of "illegitimate" and it's just not fitting, not at all.

I've grown to dislike when people ask me, "Do you talk to the mother?" I tell them, "Yes, I talk to myself all the time." I don't like hearing, "You're such a good person for adopting," or, "They're so lucky." I always have a strong urge to reply, "No asshole – *I'm* so lucky." I'm not doing charity – they are my children, my heart and my soul. I, too, gave birth to them. They were born in my heart, we were joined by destiny, and our love for one another is unconditional. I now just chalk it up to ignorance and consider those people who just don't get it to be nothing more than ignorant people. I just remind myself, as I remind my children, always consider the source.

I wasn't able to technically birth them myself, yet with every ounce of my spirit, I believe that if I had birthed my children entirely on my own, the exact same babies would have emerged from me. I understand how biology and genetics and all of that work, but none of that matters one bit. There's no convincing me otherwise. Before I even thought to ask God for them, they had already been given. I knew that my children, my soul mates, would find their way to me.

There was a picture taken of me and my husband prior to our wedding day, on the day, years ago at our co-worker's wedding reception where it had all began. In the background was a little boy walking behind us in the frame. I hadn't noticed him at the time, but seeing the picture after my son was a little older, I would swear that it was him back there. He was the spitting image of my little boy, and I'm convinced that it had been a sign. My daughter looks and acts like a mini-me, and my son and I have so many parallel traits and similarities to when I was younger – we even have similar birthmarks.

They had been my children before they had even been conceived, before I had even known that I would ever want children – as far back as then. Our route and the method of delivery we took to arrive at one another may have been unconventional – but we were going to come together one way or another. My children… truly, they are my soul mates, and I am theirs.

I have never hidden my children's background from them. I have always felt that this was their story, too. I even wrote them a story once and made it into a little book about how we became a family. I would always tell them, "Mommy's tummy didn't work, but God still found a way to bring you to me. You were both born in my heart".

Chapter 17:

Open and Shut

Chapter 17: Open and Shut

As soon as my children entered this world, they engendered in me not only a desire to make sure they had the tools, knowledge and opportunities I'd never had – but also a mission to ensure that the world we lived in would be good enough for them.

My husband and I had lived in Memphis for about two years by the time we welcomed our first child. Suddenly, nothing else in the world mattered. The culture shock of my new city no longer fazed me. Everything became about my son and – later – my daughter. My children became my whole world.

While my son was attending pre-school, there were daily news headlines about a local Catholic Culprit – some creepy guy visiting Catholic schools under the pretense of seeking information as a prospective parent, but who would ultimately make off with stolen purses and gifts during the Christmas season.

Hearing about him prompted me to do some research on predators in the area, and none of what I found sat well with me – especially when I noticed that not a single person ever bothered to stop me or anyone else at the door or in the halls during school visits. Realizing I could have stolen a child and made it out of there in two seconds without anyone raising an eyebrow was not going to fly.

I had become my mother, something most women seem to dread – but for me, it felt damn good. Finally, I felt like I truly understood her. When it came to anyone messing with her children, or any harm coming our way, she would become like Mother Bear, roaring and tearing up the place. There was nothing my mother wouldn't say or do to protect me and my siblings. Once, when I was very young at the doctor's office getting routine shots, the nurse broke the needle in my leg. It was pretty much my fault – since, like all children, I hated getting shots and they didn't have very effective calming methods for dealing with irate children back then. With all my fussing and wiggling, sure enough the needle broke mid-shot, but my mother's reaction? Instinctively, she knocked the nurse out cold – and I mean full cocked fist right across her jaw, knocking her onto the floor. So that pretty much sums it up: you just don't mess with our babies. The Mama Bear instincts were in my DNA. I'm not sure if I'm that extreme. I really am more of a lover and not a fighter, but when it comes to my children, if she must, then yes, Mother Bear will come out, all right!

Immediately, I became the dean's most persistent annoyance. I had every intention of nagging him about the school's security until he got off of his butt and did something about it. We paid tuition anyway, I pointed out – how much would it cost each family to put up a gate, install a security system, and hire a security company? He appeared to have little interest in compiling the data to respond – so I went out and got it myself. I had a security firm draw up a proposal, and I presented it to him in his office a week later. By this time, I was not only a Yankee, but a damn Yankee in his eyes – bless my heart!

By that time, I was fully determined to make some changes for the safety of my children and the other children in our community – nothing else on earth mattered, not anyone's disapproving glares, and not anyone's disinclination to do anything differently than they had ever done it before.

In the midst of this whole culprit issue, I also became curious about who I would have to call if anything unfortunate ever happened to my child. I wanted to find out if there was any organization available like the one my mother had started. I discovered one that was on a mission to stop the exploitation of children, and I got in touch with the man who ran the organization. I shared with him why I wanted to get involved, and he believed so much in my enthusiasm and genuine desire to make a difference that he asked me to join the board of the organization – which meant facing individuals who had been on the board for years already.

Once again, there I was, up against the old pecking order – the newbie, the outsider – with my dreaded new ideas from the unwelcome outside. Yet by this time, not only was I used to having a target on my back, from as long ago as when I wanted to get 6th graders into Fun Night – but in this case, the stakes were way too high for me to give a damn. If I was going to have to take on adult bullies too, then they could bring it on.

For the life of me, I couldn't understand how such discord could exist within an organization geared toward making a positive impact upon the world around us. While we needed to focus on the impact we were making, these real-life Mean Girls were caught up in the politics of who should and shouldn't receive credit for what.

I didn't have time for all the bureaucratic talk about board rules, the necessity of bowing down to the president, the politics of humoring attention-starved housewives, so on and so forth. I was there on a mission for the organization itself, along with for the children and families it was in place to assist. Nothing else mattered to me in those meetings. When I believe in something, I stand behind it with all the passion I have to make it happen and make it happen the right way.

The more I accomplished for the organization, the more invested I became in doing even more – and the more the president of

the board detested any recognition I received. After I planne
gala with virtually no support from her, she declared that I was
controlling everything, trying to take everything over, causing too
much friction, and not being a team player. I had arranged to get
practically everything for free to pull off the event, brought several
power players to the table, executed the fundraiser without a hitch
– and received a feature in a couple of local magazines that helped
promote the organization. Her response to my contributions was that
I had somehow "messed up everything."

I couldn't figure out what else I could possibly do to demonstrate
once and for all the difference that I could make. I was on a mission
to get things done. I had no time for this mess. I had a job to do, so
I did it. Period.

There is a great quote by Eleanor Roosevelt that I always remind
myself of when I have to deal with these kind of people and those
kinds of situations: "Great minds discuss ideas. Average minds discuss
events. Small minds discuss people."

It took some time for me to figure it out, but what eventually became
clear was that she was angry because my pictures instead of hers were
in our local "who's who" magazines. I did not own those magazines,
nor could I control what pictures they put in them. I obviously had
zero control over what others said or did, so none of the resulting
cattiness made any sense. None of my efforts were ever about me
hogging any spotlight – I just knew how to sell people on paying
attention, taking an interest in what was going on, and making things
happen. Yes, I wanted to draw attention, and lots of it – but for our
cause and our organization.

Again, when I'm on a mission, I get behind it fully and invest my
whole self into moving things forward. I couldn't understand how this
made me guilty of anything other than giving my all to the mission

that we had all made a commitment to serve. Truthfully, the bottom line for her was that she had a problem with me getting the attention and credibility. That's what she chose to dedicate her energy to.

I soon received a phone call from her that "everyone" wanted me off the board. The president of the board informed me that I wouldn't be reinstated for another term, and she suggested that I consider resigning. I asked if she genuinely expected me to resign from something I cared so much about – especially when I believed my resignation would hurt the organization more than it would help it.

It didn't take long for me to learn that none of what she'd said was true. I spoke to other board members to inquire about any offense I'd caused, and it turned out that no one had a problem with me besides the president – at least that's what the other board members revealed to me. One woman didn't like the way things had been going lately and issued her resignation because she no longer wanted any part of it, but she made a point of telling me before she left that she believed I brought a lot to the table.

I tried to take the higher road. I made a phone call to the president and tried to mend things. I pleaded for her to just look at this whole confusion as something we simply go through in the stages of event planning. I assured her that we could get past all this and start a clean slate because, together, we could do so many great things for the organization.

A few minutes into the conversation, when everything seemed to have calmed down, I asked her if everything was alright between us. Her reply to me was, "It's not like I want you dead or anything."

It took me a moment of shock before I could recover from her words. I'd had just about enough of her and all of the drama. After that, I absolutely had no respect for her. She was just hell-bent on getting me out of the picture and out of her way. I hung up the phone and tried to convince myself that it was all going to be fine.

Clearly everything was not okay. As if I needed further proof, I soon received a phone call from the woman I had considered to be my closest friend, in whom I had confided in about all this, who was now meekly informing me, "I can't be your friend anymore."

I was floored. That's what little kids do – we were in our 30's! Never in my life, even as a child, had I heard anyone say anything so silly to me, well, maybe once when I was 4 years old - but really?!?! I later found out that she had been going back and forth between humoring me and appeasing the president of the board – and suddenly she was faced with the decision of where her loyalty would lie. It was a catty, girly mess at its best. I didn't have time for this when we were all supposed to be working for a cause greater than ourselves. Most importantly, I was supposed to be dealing with mature adults. The way that they acted was scary because these "mean girls", these "adults?" gave birth to children and they were raising children, but yet they could not control themselves enough not to act like children. It was scary because these same "mean girls" were on boards that help children. I think I made my point.

The truly sad thing was, as I told the president, that none of this should have been about her or me. It should have been about the organization. Unfortunately, in the end, it was only the organization and the children it was looking out for that wound up hurt by all this catty mess she had created.

I appreciate a pat on the back for a job well-done like anybody else, but it was obvious I wasn't going to get one from this bunch. Still, I knew I didn't deserve – and certainly hadn't expected – the kinds of punches that came my way. But that's life, or I'm told, and that's business. It all comes down to whether you stand up and punch back – or pick up your panties and move on.

For a while, it was like I was wearing a scarlet letter. As I became involved with other organizations, these "mean girls" were issuing warnings against working with me. They urged other non-profits to "beware," claiming that they feared for their organizations. I responded by killing them with kindness every time I saw them. I continued to attend every function and gala, I still wore the same smile I always had, and I still treated everyone with the same cordiality.

That period of my life definitely demanded that I put on some pretty high stilettos, hold my chin up high, walk tall, and dare not stumble. Taking the higher road can be difficult, but it does pay off. It means a lot to me to be able to look in the mirror, know where my heart is and love who I see.

I am pretty sure my attitude and my impact spoke louder than the rumors and attacks against me. I found that the boards of other organizations wanted me and decided to take a chance anyway. It took time, but after they found out how different people's ideas were about me when they sought out recommendations for me on their own. They were smart enough and mature enough to find out the real truth and it became clear what the lies were all about. Some of these board members suggested that I take legal action against the women who were so dedicated to tarnishing my professional reputation. I opted to keep my focus on matters that truly deserved it. I later understood that their lives were miserable, their husbands cheating on them and so many other issues, so there you have it.

Later, an opportunity to help out with fundraising for a well-known children's hospital fell into my lap, and I organized an event for a separate sister organization to help their cause. Soon, another scandal was afoot – I started hearing rumors about myself supposedly having an affair with the head of the board of the children's hospital.

Once again, I was on a mission to aid an important cause that I believed in with everything in my spirit – and once again I had to deal with all this extra craziness. Once again, I was asked to resign. Really?! I mean WTF?!! Once again, it was all because of jealously and pure catty nonsense, I thought to myself, *I've been through this before, and I refuse to go through this again. Just strap on the stilettos and move forward. There is no time to be a sissy or deal will silly crap like this.*

A friend and I began noticing that every weekend, everyone we knew was attending one gala or another. They were buying new dresses for each one as if the fashion police would arrest them for sporting the same outfit twice – so we came up with an idea to start our own charitable organization.

Each year, our organization would put to use the dresses we had all dismissed, in order to brighten the spirits of young local princesses. Dress-up and tea parties were organized at the elite Peabody Hotel. The idea grew into a non-profit organization that partners with other non-profits each year to make a substantial difference in the life of at least one princess in need.

Created out of the sum of our negative experiences, the organization we formed showed me that something positive could evolve from anything if I was determined enough to stay positive, focus on silver linings, make waves, and find my "yes".

The other chaos that lead me to that victory was all just a part of life and business doing exactly what life and business tend to do. It's not easy to deal with all the lies and negativity that people with ill will and motives try to throw at you, hoping to interfere with what you're after and trying to make you stumble in your stilettos. Still, as always, one door shuts and another one opens...(even if you have to get back up and kick that sucker open, all by yourself).

Chapter 18:

Confronting Demons

Chapter 18: Confronting Demons

Well, here was the real catch: moving to Memphis actually meant being closer to his mom and closer to the reality of her becoming more of a factor in our relationship much more regularly, and much more noisily. This woman had hardly been tolerable when we had over 500 miles between us. Now, the odds were totally against me. Leaving my own entire family behind in Chicago meant that I no longer had anyone in my corner, no one in my midst to lend me an immediate shoulder. But there are some things we do in the name of love.

Out of respect for my children and the understanding that they needed to know their family, I set aside my personal resolution to keep as much distance as humanly possible between my monster-in-law and me. I wanted them to know what a family was, and if that meant trying again, trying harder to pick up all those broken pieces among us, then so be it.

After my son was born, we paid the monster-in-law – ahem, his grandmother – a visit. Her husband didn't even want me in the house. When I asked him why, he replied, "Because you're not a good person." I had no idea what I had supposedly done this time, to that family of finger-pointers always blaming someone for something. Again, I had to remember to consider the source and during that time their marriage was almost at its end as well.

It was a tendency that had reared its ugly head within the politics of my own household. Any problem I didn't fix – whether I was responsible for it or not – became my fault. Then we'd also have to argue, and *that* became my fault. And then his mother, so conveniently located now, would get involved and things would spiral even more out of control.

Someone made the comment that his mom – was just an energy vampire. She would suck all the energy out of me. In the early stages of our union, it was only when she was around that my husband and I seemed to always fight.

In front of everyone else, she would treat me like we were best friends so that I would look like the crazy one, similar to the way my ex had treated me. Anytime I was on television or in print somewhere, like in one of the who's who magazines, she loved me to pieces – suddenly, she made me sound like I was the best daughter-in-law in the world when she spoke to her friends about me. In public, she would brag and glorify me as such a wonderful daughter-in-law, someone that she simply adored. But behind closed doors, I was never treated with respect. That was her game. The rules and the object are still unclear to me. I only understood that if she could manipulate and control someone eliciting the attention and treatment she craved, she would get along just fine with them. Otherwise, there was not a chance. It was clear there was no chance written in the stars for us.

I know that no one's perfect, that we all make mistakes and that I'm no exception – but our children deserve nothing less than for us to try our best to come as close to perfection as we possibly can. I'm not Mother Teresa or the Dalai Lama, but I can damn sure do my best. One of the greatest challenges of my life has been trying to forgive this woman for not seeing things that way.

When she started going through a divorce, everything hit more forcefully than ever – and yet my understanding of who this woman was drastically increased.

Examining her more closely, I could perceive her ache for closeness, love, and affection – but she truly had no idea how to be less cold than she had always known. I would see her with my children, and there were a couple of times that she made my son cry because she wiped his face too hard. There were no real abusive actions or anything; she simply handled him too roughly, even while trying to offer an affectionate gesture. That was just her altogether.

She longed for attention, and even though I understood her motives, she would still piss me off with the manipulative tactics she used to gain it – especially from my children. When my husband and I wouldn't get the kids a dog, she went out and got one of her own to entice them to want to go visit her more. How ironic, especially since, decades earlier, she had snatched her own son's dog from him immediately upon arrival.

Over time, it became clear to me that she was a severely wounded woman. She had never been in a good place. She had been robbed of love herself. Since birth, she had been well acquainted with misery and had never figured out how to detach herself from it. She was in a painful marriage with a heavy drinker and emotional abuser. She was hurting inside – apart from her two sons, and two divorces down, one of which involved an ex-husband who would take his own life with a gun shortly afterward. That was the same man who told me that I was a bad person. Dysfunction and misery bred under the lies of this family. The demons that came out of this forced me to put on some stilettos that were made of titanium, and kept on stepping.

Yes, forgiveness can be one hell of a mountain to climb, but considering the source, understanding where it all comes from, can make it easier to look past the transgressions. Oh, what an emotional ordeal, what *drama* I have experienced with this family. It was a roller coaster I had to get off of because I just couldn't take the craziness anymore.

I had enough of all those demons!

Chapter 19:

This Little Light of Mine

Chapter 19: This Little Light of Mine

Just before the downfall of my marriage, before the divorce, people observing my marriage from the outside probably saw a pretty picture of a happy family. At times, it really was. I lived the proper life of a trophy wife, sure. But while it would have seemed that a woman couldn't get much luckier – I had a beautiful 6000 square foot home in a golf course community, two gorgeous children, two adorable dogs, two top of the line luxury vehicles, a chef, a nanny, a maid, a landscaping service, a service that came to pick up dog droppings in our back yard, an "allowance", platinum credit card access and the list goes on – in actuality, a woman couldn't have been more doomed.

My knight in shining armor had me up on his white horse, giving me security and everything else befitting of the life every little princess believes she wants to have when she grows up. And yet, I had the nerve to be miserable. Just because other people couldn't see my reasons didn't mean that I didn't have plenty of them.

He didn't exactly make it easy to for me to try and make this marriage work, but I suppose that wasn't entirely his fault. A lot of our problems, especially my feelings of neglect, had mostly to do with the demands of his job and his demons that were now coming to surface. I felt as though he had a choice when it came to where he ultimately prioritized his attention – that is, we didn't need to give in to the pressure of keeping up with the Joneses, maintaining a huge bank account, an impressive house and top of the line everything just to be happy together. Still, he felt as though he had no choice but to provide for our family on the most extreme levels that he could, and he would not allow himself to hear otherwise.

Our second child had encountered our lives a year and a half later. Everything seemed to be finding its place and it seemed that we were becoming happier with our two beautiful children, but then a few years later, things were really beginning to crumble in our marriage. My husband's job was suddenly going haywire. I think that's when the *you know what* really hit the fan in our marriage. He was always working and always stressed. By the time he would make it back home, he would bring all of that frustration along with him. He was up all hours of the night, making calls all over the world to handle overseas dealings with China and Japan and so on. Needless to say, this didn't help the growing strain on our marriage.

The addition of our second child brought more responsibility, and I felt like I basically had to handle that on my own. She never did sleep well, waking up every ten minutes in need of love and attention, so both of the kids would typically wake up just about every two hours. I didn't want to break my sleep cycle every time he got in and out of bed for a middle-of-the-night conference call and then, in turn, disturb his sleep every time I had to attend to the kids. It didn't make sense for both of us to be constantly disturbed as both of our sleeping schedules were always changing and interfering with one another. So I began sleeping in a room with our children, separate from my husband.

As my husband and I learned how to sleep without one another, we became more and more focused on our own concerns – him with the demands of a growing company, and me with the needs of our growing children.

So between the chaos of his schedule and the insanity of mine during this time, we slowly grew accustomed to sleeping apart. That's what first broke our bedroom routine – and eventually us – and with everything that monster-in-law was hitting us with, it ultimately broke our marriage.

Most of the time that I did spend with him, it seemed like the attention I received from him was generally negative. When I would make food, there was always something wrong with it. When I would do laundry, I was questioned about why it hadn't been done sooner. And so on, and so on.

I felt like I was constantly being beaten down emotionally. I was always wrong, as he seemed to see it. I was living with Archie Bunker or Al Bundy - I couldn't decide. He loved that show, *Married with Children*, and it was not difficult to see why – that was my husband, all day.

Still, I tended to feel like anything was better than when he ignored me completely, so I began doing everything I could to get his attention whenever I felt neglected. Even if it was negative attention, it was gratifying that he was paying me any attention at all, and over time, this all became the major factor of the dynamic of our marriage and of my family. I was giving into the dysfunction and falling into the trap of misery myself.

I did spend money on things for the house, for our children and for odds and ends for myself, and I was always honest with him about it. He would tell me that it was fine for me to spend it, but I could tell when it bothered him anyway. It was a way for me to get his attention after feeling overlooked for too long. It was a way for me to get back at him for all of my hurt feelings. It was the only way I knew to hurt him, to get him to pay attention to what was going on - with me, with us… to let him know that I was unhappy.

It wasn't like we were hurting for money in any way.

If I told him, "I want this," or "We need that," as usual, he would tell me to go ahead and get it, just put it on the credit card – and then, as usual, every time the credit card bill came, there was a fight about it. He would yell at me for doing things he had just given me permission for, and then I would have to bring up the conversation again to defend myself.

Any little bit of happiness that I had with him was being destroyed. Knowing of his past, I thought that I had enough in me to show him a better way, a way of love. But the more I spent trying to show him that love, the more I felt like he would never be able to see past his upbringing.

I started to feel that I would forever be the enemy, for he feared that I was going to weaken him with love. With the children, he was able to show affection but as us stay-at-home moms do, I was really the one raising them. He had work and work always on his mind all the time. I felt all I was in his life, was just another business deal.

True character often shows itself when circumstances are toughest. So, in that sense, could I blame him for being stressed and saying mean things. When I fought back, I felt that I had to be just as mean, which ultimately did not help the situation. So who was right, and who was wrong? I didn't know then, but I know now that the answer to both question is: it was both of us.

I would look at what this man had been through, and I would think, "Okay, this is why." But why was I compelled to try to go back and try and fix everything? It's the nature of a woman, I guess. And what I learned in my past. It was the pressure I had put on myself and it had definitely been a choice of mine. Truthfully, there was no way that I could blame him for everything.

The only thing I could try to do was to deliver. I was determined to show him how great life could be. Meanwhile, there was always a part of me screaming, "Love me! Let all your pain and hurt melt away. You don't need that with me in your life..." I wanted to hang in there for the sake of our family, to show him what a family truly could be and should be.

He was difficult to take during that time, but he was not always all that bad. There were always little reminders of his softer side, although he was careful to keep it tucked behind a fortress more times than not. One saddening example of that tendency occurred several years into our marriage, when I was out of town with our children and got a phone call from him sobbing uncontrollably. It was the first time I had ever heard him cry, devastated because our dog, Spaz, had died.

We had gotten Spaz together 15 years earlier, before we were even married. He was a little black pug, and he and my husband were adorable together. When we first got him, he only weighed about 2 pounds, so my husband was a sight to see, this giant, mean-looking tyrant walking around with this precious tiny creature.

He hadn't even wanted a dog. He had gotten Spaz because of me. After I heard the story of how much it had hurt him as a child when his mother took away the new dog his father had given him, I declared that he needed to finally get one after all those years. In no time at all, he fell head over heels for this dog.

On this hot summer day, our A/C units had gone out, so it was unbearably hot in the house. When my husband went upstairs to tinker with the A/C units, he didn't even realize the dog had followed him – so when he saw him, he was startled and instinctively yelled, "Spaz, get downstairs!"

My husband has a booming voice, on that is capable of putting the fear of God into any and all that are subjected to it. Spaz was so startled and overwhelmed with fear that the poor, alarmed dog shot down our wooden stairs – no carpeting – so fast that he stumbled and slid down the steps, slamming smack into the door at the bottom. With blood all over his shirt, my husband rushed Spaz to the vet only to be told that the dog wasn't going to survive. His neck had been broken, and there was just too much damage. On the phone, filling me in, my husband was inconsolable.

There were moments that reminded me it was never personal with him – I felt it was simply the way he was, and had always been, because it was the only way he had learned love. Spaz's death hadn't been my husband's fault, by any means, but it was a very real and poignant example of the kind of impact his rage could have – what it could feel like being in his presence in the wrong place, at the wrong time, when his mood was involved.

When you love, you have to let go of all of yourself, and I later realized that maybe my husband was never able to do that because of all the hurt he had felt in his life. There was a lot of deep-seeded hurt in that man, and despite of my attempts to chip away at it for all of these years, I felt that I could not convince him to forget that promise he made to himself, not to open himself up to any further hurt from anyone.

Our shared unhappiness grew to be overwhelming. We grew apart, but still kept living together, constantly attempting to construct a life that seemed to be intended more for other people than for ourselves. I wasn't happy. That's the bottom line.

I think back often to the Valentine's Day right before we had gotten married, a time when life seemed to be simple and normal. I remembered being at our friends' house. They were a married couple with two children, and they were fighting about something trivial. It was kind of funny to me at the time. The man had gotten so angry at his wife that he threw bananas on the ground in his fury, and my husband and I laughed and laughed about it once we'd gotten in the car to head home. We promised each other, after witnessing that together, that we would never be that way, and that no matter what – whether it was, Valentine's Day or any other day, we would always remember to show one another how much we loved and cared for each other. We promised to never be angry with each other on special occasions and to always, at the very least, remember to give one another cards.

Here we were, so many years later, and those promises were nothing like the reality we were living. I would still tear up thinking of that day. If we had only kept those promises, it would have made a tremendous difference in our lives and in our marriage. I missed those innocent times so much.

We did make some feeble efforts to save our marriage. We went to marriage counseling, and I clearly recall our answers when the counselor asked, "On a scale of 0-10, how likely is it that your marriage will work"

He said 8. I said 3.

My rating of 3 didn't stem from my lack of desire to try. I gave a 3 simply as an acknowledgment of the reality that my husband was not going to change.

My children definitely helped to bring me through the toughest of times – making crafts with them, watching cooking shows with them, mimicking chefs in the kitchen with them… those were the moments that trumped all others. We hired a nanny to help out since I didn't have my mom or my sister around, or anyone that I could call on when I needed help, but I was so hands- on that I drove her crazy. She put up with me though, and we soon became friends. Truthfully, I wanted her to be a part of my family, in this place where I didn't have anybody. Sure, I had those so-called friends, who turned out not to be friends after all, but she became something like my Corrina Washington, from the movie, *Corrina, Corrina*. To this day, she remains as family to me and my children. I can't imagine those years without her, how utterly alone I would have felt.

I constantly watched Desperate Housewives episodes, the ones I could get to before my husband deleted them, anyway, because I felt like I could relate. My world had begun to feel like some weird cross between their lives and the lives of the Stepford Wives – there was way too much drama, yet not nearly enough differentiation. And in my marriage, I felt that I could find no solace.

I felt like we had moved to Memphis and gotten caught up in this who's-who kind of world – and I was getting to see who was who, all right. All I'd been trying to do was find my way and fit in somewhere, and after I finally did – by helping out with causes concerning the wellbeing of women and children – I started feeling like I might not belong in my own home.

My understanding of who was who grew stronger with every passing year. I was one who was focused on letting my light shine and encouraging others to do the same, but too many of the people around me were those who had seen their own lights flicker out and couldn't wait to see whose light they could get to burn out next.

This little light of mine, I refused to let it burn out.

Chapter 20:

What's Love Got to Do With It?

Chapter 20: What's Love Got to Do With It?

Imagine standing right at the edge of a cliff. Knowing you're about to jump, having no idea what's going to happen next. No net. No harness. No spotter. I had to take this risk in order to save what was left of me, and to salvage what I could of my family. I was dying inside anyway. I felt like the risk of death was the only way to stand any chance of survival. I remembered a quote in that movie that Morgan Freeman starred in called *The Shawshank Redemption*, that had something to do with you either get busy living or dying. It spoke to me, poignantly and repeatedly.

For me it was a piss or get off the pot moment. I was standing at a fork in the road, and I knew it. My heart heavy and my soul depleted, I left home to visit our bank and an attorney. I didn't get anything in order first. I just decided that it was time to get busy living, and so I went.

I felt like a zombie that entire day. It was the early part of December, the month of Christmas. I remember thinking, *"How can I do this now?"* But I couldn't take it another day, truthfully, there is no good time to file for divorce.

I was numb as I called a friend I knew, a divorce attorney, and told her that I was coming in to her office. On the way, I stopped at the bank and learned that our account – which had contained over $120,000 only the week before – now contained just around $8,000. I didn't know what was going on, but I only needed $5,000 to draw up divorce papers. I asked the teller for a cashier's check.

When I got to my attorney, she asked me, "Are you sure?" I told her, "I have my check – please, go do it now." I was worried that if I didn't act fast, I might not go through with it. I needed her to hurry and make it official, to prove that I wasn't just going through the motions, to leave no option but for me to follow through.

She told me that the papers would be served by a third party, but I told her that – I didn't want it done that way. I would want to tell him myself. It seemed more dignified, for both of us. Having him "served" by some third party just didn't seem right. I didn't want to be public about it. I had no desire to embarrass him. Hell, I didn't even really have the desire to go through with a divorce.

The primary reason that I had come into this friend's office was that I knew that she would understand my needs and protect me and my family through whatever might come next, not try to damage us more. All that I really wanted to happen next was for him to finally understand – to wake up and decide that he wanted and needed to fight for me, for our family.

I had gotten to a point where I was just so damn mad and I was not going to take it anymore. I had to go and file. I had no idea what was going to happen, but more than anything, it was simply a cry for help, the truest test I could give us – a last resort effort to get a reaction out of him, to stir him to action. All I was really trying to say was, "Look! Our problems are real! Let's fix this! Stop the craziness! Please! Fight for me! Fight for our family!"

I felt like it was the only way to wake him up and let him known that I was serious about all the things I had been saying to him for months, for years even. We needed to grow up and I wanted him to want to fight for us, for our family. Not for his mother. Not his job. For *This*.

I wanted him to decide that we were worth it – that I was worth it… that, come to think of it, maybe he did love me after all.

He didn't.

Even later when I said to him outright, he wouldn't budge. I said to him, "So what, it cost $5,000 to file? It can cost this or it can cost thousands more in court. You can stop this. If you cared about this family, you would stop this. Right now."

He wouldn't.

I had known that, at this point, our truth would have to come out once and for all, and it sure did. Would he fight for me and our family? The answer was a resounding, "No. Not at all."

The most he had to say about his position was, "I would rather give it all to the attorneys than to give it to you."

He should have done everything in his power to save us. He could have said to me, "Let's not do this," and we wouldn't have. But that never happened.

His words, when I visited his office, standing at his desk, telling him I filed, were simple, cold, and painful. I remember them exactly, because they cut me like a knife: "Why couldn't you tell me this over the phone?" He glanced at his briefcase, and then his computer. I couldn't understand why, but he looked nervous. Then he became impatient and distraught, saying he had work to do. He asked me to leave.

No, it was not the reaction I had hoped for, not at all.

Chapter 21:

Sink or Swim

Chapter 21: Sink or Swim

I cried all the way home, and called to ask our nanny to stay late that night. She understood. I needed someone there. I didn't want to be alone with him when he came in. I knew he was going to be a monster to deal with, but I was used to that. I don't know why I was so nervous.

He was livid when he got home that night, as expected. I remember him screaming that he would ruin me. He genuinely believed that I would crumble, that I couldn't take care of myself or our children. I think that he literally wanted to take every dime, to break me down, to teach me a lesson about dishonoring him, and to show me that I needed him – that my life would be impossible, unbearable without him.

I didn't care what difficulties lay ahead for me. I had absolutely no idea what I was going to do next. I screamed back at him that I would flip burgers - not that there was anything wrong with that, I was simply proving my point – I would work, I would do anything, anywhere – before I would continue putting up with a miserable marriage like ours.

I hadn't made any plans or even set funds aside for a rainy day. I had simply given myself an ultimatum: sink or swim.

Everyone from my husband's attorney to our so-called friends added fuel to the fire, ripping us apart even more. The neighbors scrutinized me, watching my every move and noting my every encounter to report back to him or just to gossip about me. His ex-boss – a guy who would soon be heading to jail for tax fraud – from what I later found out, it was rumored, that he offered to hide money for my husband. I just did not know what to believe or what was all going on. All I knew, I just wanted this all to end. I could hardly trust anyone and I just wanted to get away from all of the drama.

I asked myself, *"Does it have to be "his team" or "my team"? Can't it just be "Team for the Kids"?* Just because a piece of paper declares divorce that doesn't mean that a family is over. We still needed to focus on doing the right thing – if by no one else, then by our children. It seemed so strange to me that the very people who had brought us to Memphis, offering to treat us like their family, were so content in helping us destroy our own family. But, I know, I need to consider the source.

The only other person who seemed genuinely concerned about the state of our family was our nanny. In fact, that remained to be the case even after she was no longer officially our nanny, after my husband had gotten rid of her and everyone else who had helped us around the house. Even when she was no longer receiving a paycheck, to her, it was about family. She continued to be there, not only to help out with the kids, but also to morally support me. To this day, she remains a major part of our lives, and I believe she always will.

During that time, she was just about all I had. I had no family anywhere near by, and my husband had uninvited my parents from our house for the holidays to punish me. He said that he didn't feel like "Mr. Happy Christmas" guy and he didn't feel like dealing with any guests.

On that Christmas day, my husband and I got into another particularly wretched shouting match. I was ready for him to get out of the house, but he had been refusing to leave ever since the divorce papers were filed. He insisted that since I was the one who had filed, if I wanted to be away from him so badly then I could just as easily be the one to pack my things and go. This was *his* house anyway, he would often point out. But he would then insist that I couldn't take the kids with me… so I couldn't bring myself to go anywhere.

I remember, in the heat of that argument, beginning to say, "You know, out of fifteen years—" when he interrupted me and exploded out of anger: "Fuck fifteen years! You've been a piece of shit for fifteen years!"

It was on Christmas Day.

The only thing I could say was, "You know what? Merry Christmas to you too."

Fortunately, the kids were already packed into the car to go and visit his mom's. So, they did not have to hear that craziness. I stayed behind and cried while I packed up our decorations, reflecting on our last "Merry Christmas" together.

The day that my attorney and I finally got him out of the house, it became instantly clear that I was in no danger of sinking. The fear, the dread – all of that which had weighed down on me for the past fifteen years of our wedded anti-bliss – vanished as abruptly as he did.

I still had to figure out where I would go from there. I reflected on the mother who had never driven, the grandmother who had never written checks, and the younger version of myself who had sworn she'd never be as dependent on her man as they had been on theirs. I realized that was exactly where I had found myself for the past fifteen years, but there was no time to sweat it at this point.

A friend of mine asked me once why, when women get divor
there has to be a whole crisis, transformation and rebirth to go along
with it. Truthfully, I wanted to punch him when he asked me that.
In marriage – and especially in unhealthy marriages – women have
a tendency to lose their power. During the divorce and afterward,
we're trying our best to gain that power back.

Another friend of mine also made a great point – why do people even
use the term "mid-life crisis"? Why not just call it an adjustment?
We're all just figuring this shit out. Every single one of us. Every
single day of our lives.

Finally, for the first time in years, I felt up to the task. My head was
clear, my spirit was lifted, and my energy was restored. Sure, I had a
long way to go, but the single most overwhelming obstacle had been
cleared from my path.

I had no doubt then that I would be strong enough to swim.

Chapter 22:

Let Him Live

Chapter 22: Let Him Live

Little had I known, my husband had already been consulting with one heck of a dirty attorney since long before I'd ever even filed – six months before, as a matter of fact, as he later admitted to me. Word on the street was that this was the lawyer that men went to because he's the one they could count on to take their wives down. He had already advised my husband to get rid of our nanny, along with any other hired help and extraneous expenses so that they wouldn't be factored into what he must continue to provide for me after we divorced.

I understood now, though, that my husband had already been setting the wheels in motion for quite some time. My actions had been impetuous, to protect my spirit; his actions had been calculated, to protect his money. My attorney broke it down clearly for me, saying, "This is going to be business for him and emotional for you."

It began to make sense why, when I'd served him the papers at his office, his immediate reaction had been to glance instinctively at his briefcase and computer. He had still been trying to figure out how to move his money around before he filed for divorce – I think he had realized I had beaten him to the punch and it meant he needed to hurry up about it. I am not sure he never anticipated that I might actually file for divorce myself but he sure was preparing for it.

From silly antics like asserting that I, who asks for cranberry juice in a martini glass when I'm at a bar so I can feel like a big girl, was an alcoholic who didn't take care of my children, to hiring a private investigator to trail me and uncover all the "dirt" that he was stunned to learn I wasn't doing, he and his lawyer were equipped non-stop with ploys, set-ups and scare tactics. Thankfully, my numerous character references from friends, colleagues and associates helped me to combat them all in the end.

One of my friends had told me to be careful, guaranteeing that my husband was going to get one of those snaky lawyers, just like every other divorced man in his circle had before him. I vehemently denied it. We had laughed together in the past about how ridiculous the people we knew looked – hiring private detectives to spy on one another and whatnot – so sure we would never wind up that way. For some reason, I still thought my husband was above all that.

Unfortunately, my friend had been right. My husband's lawyer cared nothing about our family. Between all the games he and his lawyer were playing, it was exhausting. The two of them tried relentlessly to wear me down into agreeing to some arrangement or another that wouldn't have been fair to me – and in the heat of all our "negotiations" concerning the terms of the divorce, there did come a point when I wanted so badly to just give into, sign the papers and be done with it. If it meant less than half of what I knew he had, none of the investments, and a crummy apartment in the seediest part of town, then so be it, I found myself thinking.

But then I thought of my children, and I reminded myself that I had to stick up for us. I did deserve fifty percent of everything, I never worked and I had to take care of me and the kids and I was walking away with no less. Out of anger, he claimed that I didn't deserve anything because he'd had everything we were fighting over long before we were married – but after fifteen years, two children, and being forced to stay at home, damn right, I wanted what was fair! I did not have a prenup!

Meanwhile, every new meeting with our attorneys was breaking my heart into a million new pieces.

And then, in the midst of these days, came a moment of the purest irony.

My husband had always been such a tough guy, turned off by any remote sign of weakness. He detested it in others, and didn't allow it in himself – he was a real "no pain, no gain" kind of man's man, which was why he'd always had such a hard time putting up with me any time I had a panic attack.

Yet one early morning, my phone rang; it was my husband, in agony. He told me that he couldn't breathe.

This man – the man who had scoffed with annoyance at my every single panic attack and hospital visit, who had spent every day of the past several months openly declaring his intention of "ruining me" – still considered me as the person he could count on most in his time of need. I – this woman he hated so much, who had been "a piece of shit for fifteen years" – was the one he first thought to call for help.

That morning my character was tested like it had never been tested before. That morning, I discovered what I was truly made of.

With no other choice, I rushed the kids over to my next door neighbor's house and then hurried to his apartment. My head was spinning during the entire drive. "What if he's dying? Would I save him? Should I save him? If – God, forgive me – but if something were to happen to him, all this fighting would end. I would get everything. I would have peace." I dwelled, for some time, on all his stomping around and endeavoring to crush me.

And then, as I turned the corner to get to his apartment, I pleaded with God while crying, "Please, let him live." I told God that I would put up with everything else my husband had in store for me – that I didn't know why things were happening the way they were, but that my children needed their father no matter what.

When I got to his apartment, he opened the door but was having such a hard time breathing and he was in pain, I told him to lie down on the floor. I did not know what to do but I told him to lie on his side because I didn't know if it was a heart attack. He only knew that he was in severe pain.

It felt like it took forever for the ambulance to get there, and he was in so much pain by the time they did – rocking back and forth in agony, still having trouble breathing.

At the hospital, we found out that he was passing kidney stones. For a man, that was a pain probably even worse than childbirth.

Here was a man who had never experienced real physical pain like that before. If anything felt physically awry, he'd refuse to visit a hospital. The fact that he'd come this time without protest spoke volumes about the agony he was suffering.

Thinking back now, I realize that this whole episode could have been a real "nanner nanner nanner" opportunity for me. But I wasn't even thinking about all that then. At the time, I was just scared. There was something terribly disconcerting about watching this supposedly impervious force feel such pain and experience such weakness for the very first time.

And then things got worse. The doctor gave him some pain killers, medicine to help him bear the pain as he passed the kidney stones, but he had some allergic reaction to the pills. His vital signs monitor began displaying what I thought were sporadic flat-lines, and I frantically ran out to the nurses to tell them something was wrong. Four or five of them came rushing into the room.

Again, I begged God to please let him live.

I had never imagined that I might ever put so much hope into a person who had shown me such ill will. And yet I even found myself thinking that if this man lives, it will be these moments that determine whether or not we're supposed to be together. If anything would bring us back together – show us what we meant to one another, prove that we could prevail as a family – it would be this. I wasn't banking on it... but I have to admit that the thoughts did cross my mind.

The nurses got his vitals back to normal, and afterward I padded him down with washcloths. I kissed him on the forehead, vowed that I was there for him, and prayed for God to take care of him.

And then things got more interesting. God certainly does work in the strangest ways.

While I was waiting out in the family room as my husband was still recovering, a nurse brought all his belongings out to me – his iPhone, his Blackberry, and his keys were included. I was still his wife, after all.

I really had never snooped through his phones before then, but I couldn't resist the opportunity planted right there in my lap – not with all the plotting and scheming he and his lawyer had been putting me through.

What I found in his cell phones were some answers I needed. The answers I will keep private.

My husband was on meds and needed someone to take care of him. So I brought him home with me and the kids.

I thought for sure that after all this had transpired, the fighting would be over – at least for a little while. Hell no. The next day, when he was feeling better, he was back in his attack mode and on the phone with his attorney. So much for that fairly-tale ending.

When we finally went to mediation, they didn't let us in the same room. I never understood that, but I guess it was for the best, considering all the contention between us. In my pocket, I had my spiritual trinkets – my cross and my St. Michael. In the middle of it all, I asked to speak privately with my husband. The attorney told me that we were near an agreement and warned me that I didn't want to mess anything up or complicate things by getting into some argument, but I felt like I had to speak to him.

I told him about what I found in his phones and asked him to tell the truth about everything. The exchange was like an elixir. We made amends right there, for the purposes of our negotiations anyway. We went back inside, and he did things fairly.

Whatever those answers did, I felt that they had given me power, leverage – I felt it was something I could use against him to make him do the right thing. When it was said and done, in some sense, it was a victory for me, but not really, because who ever really "wins" in divorce? It had taken us a year and several months for us to get this process behind us. But finally, the healing could begin and the both of us lived.

Chapter 23:

Dangling Toxic Carrots

Chapter 23: Dangling Toxic Carrots

As I thought back over the past several years, so many things were beginning to make sense.

The weekend before our first Thanksgiving in Memphis – three weeks after we had moved to our new city – I had woke up around 11:30 one night with heart palpitations. I spoke my husband's name, shaking him to wake him.

He had snatched his arm away, "What?"

He had been angry at me for disturbing his rest – he had a big week coming up at work.

I'd told him it was hard for me to breathe, that my heart felt like it was pounding out of my chest, that I was worried that I was having a heart attack.

"You're fine," he'd told me. He hadn't opened his eyes once.

"I need to get to the emergency room."

"You just need to calm down."

He'd sat up in the bed, and then abruptly stood to leave. I asked where he was going, and said, "I'm up now. I'm going to work on my report."

He'd insisted that nothing was wrong. "Just lie there," he'd said. "You'll be fine." And he'd left, just like that.

I had never felt so abandoned. I couldn't scream. I couldn't explain. I couldn't get up. I couldn't do anything but what he'd told me to do before he walked out – lie there – while I felt like I was waiting to die.

While in bed, helpless, staring at a picture of my grandmother and grandfather in a frame on our dresser, I had pleaded for them to be my guardian angels and had asked God to let me live. And under their loving gaze, I had made it through the night.

When I woke up in the morning, I still wasn't feeling quite right, but I had enough strength then to call my doctor – who told me that I should have gone to the hospital the night before. Next time, he'd said, I'd better get to the emergency room immediately.

All that my husband had to say after I told him about my doctor visit was, "What do I know? I'm not a doctor." I felt he had no remorse, no regret, no consolation. Unacquainted with the idea of weakness of any kind, he simply had no respect for another person's pain. He had never allowed himself to acknowledge any. He had no basis for empathy.

As far as what had been wrong with me, the doctor couldn't say for certain. As a precaution, he took me off my thyroid medication, which does have possible side effects of heart palpitations and anxiety, despite his assessment that there was no reason that it should have awakened me in the middle of the night in that way. I had also taken cough medicine that night for my cold, although I usually stay away from chemical intake altogether – from meds to alcohol, the idea of putting chemical substances into my body always made me uncomfortable. Acknowledging that my body was extremely sensitive to chemical alterations, the doctor said that it possibly could have had something to do with the previous night's incident.

A month later, in January, I traveled to New York on a business venture that I'd convinced my husband to let me pursue. During a business dinner in Greenwich Village, as I turned my head to address someone at our table, my neck cracked a little. The sensation frightened me so much that my heart began beating very quickly – that all too familiar rapid pace I'd learned to dread – so I ran to the bathroom. When I returned to the table, I felt like the room was spinning. Suddenly, everyone was clearing the table and rushing me to the front of the restaurant.

The next thing I knew, this big masculine fireman entered, and my first thought when I saw him had been, *"Hubba hubba."* I'd laughed at myself, understanding that I must not be dying after all... but if my last moments on earth were going to be in the arms of this big, tall, hunky fireman, then I guessed that wouldn't be so bad. That had clearly just been my sense of humor functioning as some sort of defense mechanism because once inside the ambulance, I realized my body was shaking uncontrollably, and I had no idea what was wrong with me.

The ambulance rushed me to the emergency room and I was sent to the waiting area sitting between one person who was in the middle of a heart attack and another who was suffering from a gunshot wound, blood gushing out of his arm. The walls were yellow and dingy, packed with chaos from corner to corner. I became more convinced than ever that I was dying this time. Calming down was not a realistic option in that space.

The minute I was seen, the nurses hooked me up to the EKG's. The doctor tried giving me Valium and told me I was having a panic attack. I told him that I didn't want to take any drugs, so he told me to at least take the medicine home with me – maybe I would change my mind later. He informed me that I was in perfect health, that there was nothing medically wrong with me – but that if I wasn't going to take the meds then I really needed to relax and calm down before he could allow me to leave.

He asked what I was doing in New York and whether I was stressed about anything. I told him about my business venture, my recent move to Memphis a couple of months back, the sudden loss of my support system, the chaos my mother-in-law had contributed to that transition, and so on. He said it was no wonder that I was so stressed. There had been quite a bit going on lately.

Meanwhile, we were trying to get in touch with my husband, still in Memphis. When I finally got him on the phone, I was once again disturbing his sleep – and he was once again blatantly displeased with the disruption. Annoyed, he shouted at me, "What, are you crazy?" And just like that, fresh off my panic attack, I was arguing intensely with my husband, unbelievable, his first thought was to accuse me of being crazy before he even asked how I was feeling after such a traumatic night.

After those first couple of episodes, it had seemed like any and everything suddenly possessed the power to terrify me. Anything at all might go wrong, and I would become overwhelmingly afraid. My heartbeat would quicken… and there I was again.

It seemed that my husband began getting used to the occasional panic attacks, but he still undeniably regarded it as weakness on my part. I learned how to calm myself down by just stepping away, getting some air, and walking around a bit. Meanwhile, I was still trying to make sense of the cause of these episodes.

A few years after my first major episodes, I was awakened with my heart pounding from a bad dream, but I knew something more than that was wrong with me. I tried to relax on my own, as I had learned to do in most cases. It eventually became clear to me that I needed to go to the hospital.

During the ride to the hospital, the paramedic was like an angel, murmuring to me during the ride, "This, too, shall pass. I know you hear these words all the time, but let it go to God."

Like the time when this happened in New York, the doctor wanted to give me meds. I again insisted that I didn't need them, that I could manage to relax myself – and normally, I could... but this time, my husband kept entering the room.

He had dropped the kids off at his mother's, but then – instead of acting aloof and uninterested as he usually did during these attacks – he opted to come back to the hospital and stay by my side. It was an eye-opening experience for me, a fascinating irony. I had always figured that his presence would be comforting, reassuring. I was glad that this time, for once, he had cared enough to stay close. But every time he neared me, my nerves were racked all over again. It didn't help that he kept fussing over his Blackberry because of work, as usual. He was just such an intense person to be around.

I finally came to the realization that I needed to get away from him. I told him and my doctor that I just wanted to be alone for a little bit. I left my hospital bed and walked around for awhile outside – and that distance from my husband, that slight change of scenery, seemed to work wonders.

Once again, the doctor told me that I was in perfect health, my blood-work indicated no medical issues, and I had no family history of any condition that would cause such episodes. I told him that I had been trying to figure this out for years – I had researched anxiety, depression and beyond. The doctor suggested that I go "talk to someone."

It only took two sessions for the therapist to draw everything out of me. After looking into my medical history, he said, with finality, "Marie, it's not any medication. It's not your DNA." Then he wrote it on his whiteboard: "It's your marriage."

My husband was usually stressed because of his job, and he brought that negative energy home with him more often than not. Any chance he got, he was breaking me down because something at work wasn't going the way he wanted. If he couldn't keep things under control there, he would take extra care to run a tight ship at home. Dinner had to be on the table by 5:30, any laundry basket left unattended too long provoked questioning - why I couldn't get all the housework done when I had a nanny to help with the kids was a frequent topic of conversation – despite the fact that everything was, in fact, completed according to his timeline and our house was, in fact, always immaculate.

Still there was always something wrong. I was Martha freaking Stewart in our house, and yet he was always complaining that I never did anything right. Something I cooked wouldn't taste right. Something I did wasn't done quickly enough. Every conversation about finances became an argument. Anything he couldn't control became a shouting match. Anytime I knew he was going to address me harshly, stress kicked in big time. It reminded me of the feeling I would get as a child when I knew I was in trouble with my daddy or the principal, only double that and then some.

I felt like was damned if I did and damned if I didn't, in all matters between us, but I thought I had reached a point by then that I had ceased caring so much.

I had even thought I was happy. I could have sworn I was, especially after my children had entered the picture. Yes, I had been up against a lot of stress, and yes, I had been surrounded by a lot of negative energy. But I was thinking that is normal what everyone goes through in life during tough times. But with my vows, I had promised that we would prevail through all things.

I thought back, like I did often, to my father's words on my wedding day as the doors opened for me to walk down the aisle. He had said, "Kid… it's not always about love. It's about what you can handle."

I had insisted that I could handle it, even knowing what I knew then. I hadn't expected a fairy tale life. I had known marriage is not always easy and sometimes it would be a bumpy road. I hadn't realized our marriage would end up being a full-fledged roller coaster, but dammit – I could have sworn that I could handle it.

And so it had gone on that way for years, with little carrots dangling to keep going. Those carrots, as it turned out, had been toxic. I learned, after my divorce, that the therapist had been right after all – because since the day my husband moved out of our house during our divorce years later, I've never yet experienced another panic attack.

I had never truly comprehended, until then, what was going on in my marriage was not only very real, but also very detrimental.

It took me longer than it should have to see also the irony in my involvement with organizations aiding abused women and children: every day, I had felt like I was fighting battles in my own home – and losing. There I was, the Chair for an organization that focuses on fighting heart disease in women, and yet I was constantly towards the end, fighting this war within my own home, one that was sometimes even sending me to the emergency room. Being on those boards and a part of events that facilitated healing for others had eventually become a way of also trying to heal myself, probably long before I even realized that I had more or less been one of "those women" that our causes aimed to support.

After reminiscing about all that, with a big sigh of relief, thankfully, no more dangling toxic carrots ever again.

Chapter 24:

Closing Arguments

Chapter 24: Closing Arguments

It was a major weight off my shoulders. I was so tired of fighting, trying to get someone to realize who I was and to love me for who I was, to look at me and realize I also had a voice that counted and wasn't just an object to toss money at in an effort to make me shut my mouth. I hadn't gotten a chance yet to grieve my divorce. I'd had to spend the whole time with boxing gloves on.

Looking back, I really do think that since I moved to the South, my whole world has truly changed. The dynamic grew around me more and more of the woman staying home and putting on makeup to look the part of the pretty trophy wife. That was all my past several years had consisted of in that 6000 square foot home we kept, just as yet another way of ensuring that we kept up with the Joneses. Like the other women, I had to wait for my husband to get back home from his big important job, but after a while, that grew really tiring – the waiting and watching myself become something that I wasn't. I became sick and tired of fighting just to be who I was.

He was the one who hadn't wanted this family all along. If he really wanted to make this work like he told everyone he did, he would have fought for me. He wouldn't have instead focused his energy on avoiding all responsibility for his actions, or lack of actions, and making me out to be a horrible mother just to minimize potential alimony payments.

You could say I didn't stick around for my family either, but it was for my family that I did what I did. I had to make changes for me, for my children… and even for him.

Change is good, and when all was said and done, this was no exception. I'd needed the change. I'm sure we all did. We were all overdue for a rebirth. I needed new friends. I needed to find myself again. We needed to be apart.

No matter what anyone says, everyone heals on their own time and in their own way. There are reasons for everything. I guess sometimes things have to crumble altogether before we realize a way, or even the need, to rebuild. That was where I found myself now. The first thing I longed to do after the divorce was finalized was to get rid of this house – to sell it and finally have my very own. I felt like only then I would truly be able to move on.

It's strange, being with someone for many years and going through all these things together only to wind up apart in the end. Yet, being apart, I began to feel like I might actually be able to finally get my ex-husband and my children into a good rhythm. We started counseling and began trying to get along for them, to get things right for them.

People used to ask me if I thought that we would ever work it all out and wind up back together. I honestly think he has got so many wonderful qualities, that's why I married him. Ultimately, in the grand scheme of things, we do have a family together. He's not going anywhere and neither am I. I don't really see us getting back together, but how does anybody ever know anything for sure? I never saw myself getting a divorce. All I know is, finally, I'm comfortable in my skin. I know I don't have all the answers - nothing that truly matters comes with instructions, and even if it did, knowing me, I probably wouldn't read them anyway.

I always try to instill in my children truth, integrity, respect, honor and the right *kind* of love for a reason. I want to make sure that I teach them that there are so many levels and variations of love, some right and some wrong. Those that are right are free and unconditional, and based on truth and integrity. Those that are wrong are based on merely image, on selfish or controlling foundations, based on greed or fear.

As I learn more about myself, I learn more about what happened in my marriage. I was so young, insecure and naïve, thinking that I needed his approval and his love. I finally figured out that all the love I needed was within me. Now that I was on my own, I often had to remind myself to believe in *me*. I don't know when or where, but at some point I had stopped believing in myself in a lot of ways.

When I look back on our life together, watching the tapes of us as a loving couple growing into a loving family, there were a lot of happy moments - I wouldn't have remained married to him that long otherwise. I wouldn't have been faithful to him otherwise.

I kept recalling the few good memories that I managed to remember. I kept thinking that if only he had been able to allow himself to relax and just have fun with me instead of taking everything so seriously and trying so hard to control everything, we could have always been as fun and as free as we were on those days... no cell phone, no boss calling, no having to stay up late and talk to people overseas, no monster-in-law, no neighbors, nobody in the way of just us.

Shame on all the people who hurt my family, or any family for that matter. Shame on them for neglecting their own troubled situations and instead trying to destroy another's. All of those people who had asked me, before anything else, what church I belonged to, in actuality needed to examine their Bibles more closely. There were so many people throwing punches at our family left and right – how could we stand a chance? So many of those people who were punching at our already fragile situation were supposed to be our friends, but instead of trying to help us along, they lied and they instigated. They picked sides and they helped fuel the fire that led to our destruction. To this day, those same people claim to be his friend while they still gossip about me. Funny. Not really.

I really did try to save my marriage. I tried liking what he liked, getting involved with whatever he wanted to do and making sure he always knew that I was his number one cheerleader. We spent time with other couples, his friends, our so-called "friends". The more time we spent around them though, the more I learned that those friends of his weren't usually honest with their wives. My husband always had so many stories what they were doing but swore he was the good one.

After everything was said and done, and I learned more about the private investigator he'd had trailing me around, I wanted to see the footage he'd spent so much of his precious money on having me followed. It was such a joke, seeing myself hanging out at a restaurant, basically just having dinner with my girlfriends and clearly doing nothing wrong. There was not only footage from the time after I filed for divorce, but also footage from well before then. I truly dislike his attorney for encouraging such nonsense to enter into such a serious matter, but my husband is the one who made that choice himself and I resented him for it.

I was told I had everything, that I had been given everything. But it was never really mine. I know that I did the right thing by divorcing him because I don't think we ever had a chance, especially with so many people constantly trying to rip us apart, from neighbors to colleagues to the monster-in-law from hell.

When I look back on everything he's been through, from his upbringing, his mother, his father's absence, his job, the many stresses, the many heartbreaking things he'd been through… that was what always kept me holding on… my wanting him to know that there was more to life.

It truly is a sad story and I guess she did finally win in the end, the monster-in-law. She was able to keep battling until I had enough of her and the drama she brought into my family. The icing on the cake of my breaking point was hearing him talk on the phone with her, telling her lies about me. I'd had enough of all the games, the fake smiles, the family who loved to listen but never looked at themselves or their own faults – the epitome of jealousy, insecurity and misery at its finest. I was constantly being told that I was a bad person. Why? Because I stuck up for myself? Of course I did. I had to. If I was still there after fifteen years, it was clearly not about money. It was about building our family, our home and our life.

I feel I was probably the best thing that ever happened to him, but he couldn't even recognize that. He was so used to being unhappy because no one would ever let him be happy. What a place to put your son in, tearing his dreams and his happiness apart. I will never understand how, being a mother, you could ever rip apart your sons and their families so callously and so cold-heartedly.

Can I blame him 100 percent? No. I just expected him to be stronger. I needed him to fight for us. I don't hate anyone, but it takes a great effort not to be torn up every time I think about it all.

Regardless, we all make choices. His mother robbed him of love, yes, but then he robbed himself of love. We are all held responsible and accountable for our decisions and our actions. Our lessons will come to us in the form of consequences for everything we've done, good and bad, and now it's just all about forgiveness. Knowing his whole story was what made it was easy for me to begin to forgive him, after all was said and done.

I never felt that my husband couldn't allow himself to feel really good about anything, and I never understood why. I asked him one day, long after it was all over, why he couldn't just let go. With me as his wife for fifteen years, why did he always had to play this tough guy? Why did he listen to those neighbors, attorney and all those negative people? But it is what it is. I can't change the past. I can't change what happened. I can only deal with now. He did insist, feeling that it was important for me to know, that I was the only one. I could have had it all! How true is that? How can I ever know?

He told me recently that I was the closest thing to love he had ever experienced – and that now he's hardened even more. But he had a hand in all of it... he and that foolish pride shit. He could have put a stop to it all. It is the past and we need to forgive.

To him, my filing and our divorce all amounted to a major betrayal. Everyone in his life had betrayed him, from his mother to his boss, and I was no different as far as he was concerned. Here was the one thing in his life that was supposed to be rock solid, and I, too, had given way. I'm sure the weight of the world was on him and he had no clue what was coming or what to do when it hit, but enough had simply been enough. After fifteen years of trying to get someone to see you, to love you, to believe you're worth more than they can see... enough.

When I look back and try to see what I did wrong in our marriage, it's sometimes hard for me to see it. I think that in his eyes, it all came down to me spending too much money. That does not mean it is right but that is the fight in any marriage. Our problems had to run deeper than that. What I feel I really did wrong was argue back and say hurtful things, even when I felt I was telling the truth.

There are some things I would say back to him when I felt hurt. They were horrible things, but I know that they weren't any worse than the things he said to me. When you feel you are being abused, verbally and emotionally, you have to stick up for yourself, and that's what I felt like I was doing—sticking up for myself for years, trying to show this man a different way of life. I thought I had enough love in me to carry us both, but I was wrong.

My husband had such a booming voice that our neighbors could hear us arguing, constantly. After the divorce, they did seemed relieved. This information also comes from the ones who gossip about me. One of them had remarked, "You had a tumultuous marriage." I suppose a lot of the arguing had really been foreplay, too. We'd joke around, until… it's just the way our marriage was.

I had spent so much time reminding myself of all that, "Sticks and stones may break your bones," nonsense, but I finally started thinking to myself, *"Why the hell should I have to get a tougher backbone? Why do I have to brace myself to accept people's verbal punches? Why am I the one who needs to change? Why can't society change? Why can't people just stop being mean to each other? Why is it too much to just do the right thing and be nice to each other? Disrespect is a learned behavior, so why can't people just stop teaching it and that be the end of it?*

I really don't know what more I could have done for our marriage than what I did. I tried. I truly did try, but I could only do my best. It's all that anyone can do. I don't see that anything I did was all that awful in the end. Then again, I know he must have his own side of the story that sounds totally different from mine. Neither one of us was perfect. No one is.

I know that he must have somehow loved me in his own way - he just never learned how to show me in a way that I could understand. Somewhere down the line, I must have failed too. I allowed all the bullshit to happen that eventually became too much for me. I kept asking myself why I felt that I hadn't been strong enough to get through this with him and show him the love I wanted him to know existed, but then again, you can't control anybody. It's enough of a task to control yourself, your own mind and your own thoughts.

These were the truths I was finally faced with – and in with my closing argument…the truth will set you free.

Chapter 25:

Bat Out of Hell

Chapter 25: Bat Out of Hell

So here I was, finally divorced. I mean, it was bittersweet, after all the fighting, to finally try to find some peace and start anew somehow, to regain control over my life, to begin again making my own decisions about what to do with myself and my time without anyone over my shoulder telling me no.

I felt that feeling again, like I was standing at the edge of the cliff, knowing I'm going to jump with no idea what the hell I'm going to hit. The crazy thing about it was that, when I jumped, I landed. I landed and I took off running, running in my stilettos, even though I was afraid like you wouldn't believe. I had this new freedom. I was a woman with a purpose, a woman whose purpose had been left on the back burner for far too long – and I was ready to take the world by storm, like a bat out of hell.

I'd never had or dealt with the money the entire time I was married. I had sworn that I wouldn't be like my mother and grandmother, but I had somehow let it happen to me anyway, and now I had to figure it all out. There I was, the "man of the house", taking care of the bills. I had child support and alimony, but it wasn't nearly what I was used to – he'd made sure of that. That was okay anyway. I was not in a bad financial state and I remembered that I had lived with my mom on food stamps before, so I thought, "Who cares?" Anything had to be better than living the life I'd just left behind. Anything. I am sure most won't feel sorry for me, I am not asking for anyone to, but you shouldn't judge until you been there or truly understand everything and felt the way I did and do.

I now find it funny, because I'd been married all that time to a man who complained that I had no idea how to handle anything financially, yet here I was, able to keep a budget, pay bills and make – although a little risky – some very promising investments... all the while I was working with much less than he'd ever had to work with.

On the bright side, I had a close friend who was also a fashion designer. At least I could look like I was keeping it together, at a discount. He would say to me, "Girlfriend, you may be going through a divorce and not have the money you're used to, but who cares? You're still gonna look fabulous! You've got your Hilton!" My entire post-divorce wardrobe was Hilton Hollis, so I was still able to look the part. It was all bittersweet and scary as heck, but I knew I could make it on my own.

I knew so many women who wouldn't leave their marriages because they liked "their lives" too much. There was one who even had told me, "I like my manicures and pedicures, and if I have to blow him once in a while, who cares? I like my life." Another one had said, "I don't understand what you're doing. I like my Mercedes. All you need to do is suck it up, girlfriend." Yet another one even told me, "I'm not happy. He cheats, but I get what I want in the end anyway – a big house and big pockets."

To each her own, I thought to myself. I understood completely, but at the end of the day I had simply not been happy with my life, and now it all came down to a matter of handling my business. I did not care more about a high end car or full pockets than I did about love – the real kind. Once I understood that wasn't what I had, I couldn't allow myself to settle anymore.

Needless to say, things did change. The so-called friends I'd had no longer fit that bill. I had to start over almost completely anew. There might have been one or two stragglers among the people we had both known that stuck around. The woman next door would no longer even speak to me, although her husband remained neighborly, kindly blowing the leaves for me and helping me out with handiwork of that sort around the house. They were never the same friends I had thought they were in the past. They took his side, choosing to believe things about me, never once actually consulting me about my side of the story. To this day, they still have not had their fill of gossiping about me.

I suppose in some way it all made sense. When someone is going through a divorce, no one wants to be involved – except, apparently, those who want to be involved in all the wrong ways, adding to the turmoil. There were probably one or two good people who genuinely seemed to want to see us make it through okay, but they were the exception.

The only one still standing by my side when the smoke cleared was my Nanny, undoubtedly at this point, a true friend. She was no longer paid to work for us, but she still stuck around to be there for me and for my children, and that really proved her love. She will forever be an integral part of our family.

Generally speaking, my entire support system was in Chicago. I thought a lot about moving back there. I had, after all, only come to Memphis for my husband, but he was no longer my husband. Why not go back home?

I had to think long and hard, replaying in my mind the past several years of my life. I had to dig to find my "yes" in this place. I would have had to find it anyplace I ended up, but I felt like finding it here had been far more difficult for me than it would have been elsewhere.

In part, it seemed like a perfectly good reason to leave it all behind, yet it also seemed like just as good of a reason for me to stay put. Add to that the factor that for my kids, Memphis was home – and no matter how much easier it might make things for me and my life, I couldn't bring myself to separate them from their father.

Besides, there was so much good in this city, I was sure. It was still trying to break through, but I could tell it was on the verge. I could feel it, and I was beginning to see it.

I considered all the passion I had seen around Memphis along with all the passion I possessed within myself – my love for movies and music and fundraising – and envisioned an empire, an entertainment powerhouse. I declared to keep myself, "I'm going to make this work." That declaration gave me something to focus on to keep from falling, something I'd seen many women do in the aftermath of divorce. I was determined to figure out how to support myself and my kids and to actually do something that I loved in order to make it happen.

Risk. Uncertainty. Those are both a part of life whether you're in a healthy marriage or not, whether you have it good or not. It goes for any and all things. One day, you can have a great job and a better salary and the next day the company close, changing your whole life. You've got to suck it up and start all over. You've got to have faith and be smart. You must follow your gut and take life into your own hands. You've got to be able to put on those stilettos and boxing gloves sometimes and just fight... fight to win. It's not easy. No one ever said it would be. But it's not impossible either. No, it's not for sissies, but you can find a "yes" if you are determined. So why not take that leap to start over?

I had already been through hell and back. My hell had been watching what was going wrong in the marriage and the divorce, but now the divorce was over. I had flown out of that muck and, instead of allowing myself to fall, I was going to jump. I was on the edge of a cliff about to take a dive. When I leapt, I soared.

The seeds had already been planted, beginning several years before. It must have been my destiny.

Years earlier, my best gal pal, at that time, and I were sitting at a bar in Nashville, attending an after-party for a Poison concert - a night out I had treated her to as a pre-wedding present. It was the typical set up for a joke, us sitting there, "the blond and brunette" at the bar. We were actually hoping to meet Bret Michaels from Poison. In the meantime, there was another band performing onstage, called the Mulch Brothers.

Next to us at this bar there were these two men, bikers. One guy walks up and says, "Hey, I'm the local nut." Kind of a corny pick up line, but it was pretty unique. As it turned out he wasn't a nut after all. He knew the Mulch Brothers and offered to introduce me to his friend, Billy Falcon, who had co-written a few Bon Jovi songs along with songs for the Mulch Brothers. When I met him, I asked Billy which Bon Jovi song he had written. Only when he answered, *Everybody's Broken*, only then did I believe him. I had been waiting for him to name a really obvious and bogus hit, but you have to be a true fan and really know your Bon Jovi to be able to single that song out just off the cuff.

After that, I met the Mulch Brothers, and they gave me their CD. I told them about a Rock for Hope concert event that I was putting together on Beale Street to benefit a children's hospital in Memphis and I asked if they wanted to be a part of it.

Afterward, they were surprised by the fact that I actually followed up and did exactly what I said I would, getting in touch with them and delivering on my word to include them and get them out there. Things went pretty well with the event overall, but didn't appreciate the fact that I witnessed people deliberately not doing the right thing – namely the business pocketing more money than the charity.

Regardless, out of a horrible situation came a bright silver lining. The Mulch Brothers recognized what I was all about, and they liked it. That night, they made a pitch to me that I should be their manager. I was a little taken aback. I had never really been much of a country music fan, their genre of choice. There was another guy there courting them, but they said they liked the way I did business. I laughed it off at first, but they insisted that they were serious – that the way I am, and the way I present myself, spoke volumes and convincing them that I could make incredible things happen for them. So I took them up on it – especially after they mentioned that there weren't many women who fulfilled such roles in the industry. *Hmmm*, I thought. *Why the hell not?*

In Nashville, where they were based, I found that people really seemed to like me. They understood passion and the significance of a mission. I was meeting people and doors were opening and it was all so fast. I met a woman who had managed a very famous country singer for several years, took me under her wing. I was lucky to be learning the ropes from this powerful woman.

Nashville felt like such a breath of fresh air, that I found myself traveling back and forth from Memphis to Nashville whenever I could find time between my children's school activities. It seemed like everyone there had it all together, working toward their goals – most importantly, they were working *with* one another.

I told the Mulch Brothers to make a wish list so that we could start working our way down it getting things accomplished. They wanted a deal with a record label. I told them I wanted to do big things like get their songs put in movies. I didn't want to be the manager on the road, but I was going to do my best to make everything on their wish list happen for them. Now I was really on a mission.

I met one of the owners of Savannah Music Group, who also happens to be an owner of Voyage Air Guitar, and Halt Medical. We hit it off as friends immediately. I told him about my vision for the Mulch Brothers, along with my ideas for music publishing, and my plans for all of the Memphis talent that was waiting for an outlet. To help build that bridge more successfully, I wanted to try and bring Nashville to Memphis through Savannah Music Group. I wound up becoming an investor with them right after the Mulch Brothers were signed.

I began to have a clearer vision of my own empire that I wanted to create in order to eliminate the hurdles of labels and so many of the other crooked things I saw going on across the entertainment industry.

In the midst of all this, I got a chance to meet a film producer who lived in Memphis part-time and wanted to shoot some films here. Wanting to learn the film industry, I made sure to stay close by his side. He and his crew rented a big old house owned by an NBA player. It was like a huge bachelor pad. I got to meet actors, get some hands-on experience on a movie set, and learn the process of how a film gets made. I hung around just in case they needed anything, acting as something like an assistant because I wanted to stay around in order to learn as much as I could. If they needed to find *anything* from a cleaning service to a repair service, I was on it. They wanted to meet investors, so I started introducing them to people.

Little did I know at this time, this was not a person I could count on. He made a film here, yes, and it gave me a chance to learn a lot, sure. But in the end, there were so many issues. I started hearing rumors that there were people not getting paid – and, furthermore, the rumor about he disappeared with the money that was raised for a second film that never actually got made. From what I understood, lots of lawsuits and plenty of craziness ensued as a result.

While all of this was going on, I met a line producer, who had gotten hired on. Out of what turned out to be a horrible situation, our meeting had turned out to be a silver lining. I told him my vision of creating an entertainment powerhouse composed of a film, a music and management company all under one roof. He and his cronies didn't think it was possible, but they were entertaining my ideas anyhow to humor me. I told him I wanted for one of the Mulch Brothers songs to be in the movie he was working on, and I asked him what was the best way to break into this industry. He told me that I could always put skin in the game, meaning, to put funding into a project.

So I invested in his film, called *Momo: The Sam Giancana Story*, and began learning even more about the business. I called him my Obi-Wan. I learned so much from him and through him, observing everything he had to go through to pull off his project.

I brought on other investors to *Momo* and, meanwhile, began pursuing other endeavors, and representing some other acts in the music industry.

I was lucky enough to get to go backstage when one of the artists I was working with opened for Bon Jovi a couple of times, and I had a chance to meet Bon Jovi's management team. I was meeting so many well-known actors and musicians, and they often acted as mentors and advisors to me. I rode the wave of those and other great opportunities, and once *Momo* was finished, it was time for film premiers. Then it was on to the next project with that producer.

I wanted to find a place to launch the foundation of my vision. I started knocking down doors – kicking them in with my stilettos is what I like to say – trying to get investors for my other film projects, my big vision.

Basically, I broke out of the cage, like a bat out of hell.

Chapter 26:

Getting My Groove Back

Chapter 26: Getting my Groove Back

After I filed for divorce, I had somewhat of an emotional affair. He was really just a good friend that helped me along with his moral support, someone who took me by the hand and said, "You are beautiful. You do not let anybody do this to you." I called him Romeo… A brief affair was sparked later after the divorce, but truly nothing much or serious would really ever come of it because of my standards. He loved to date many women and, because I don't want to date anyone who has dated half the world, it would have never worked. But he helped me a lot, uplifting me while I was going through it all. My Romeo… We've kept in touch since then, and he remains a very good friend to me even to this day, one I will never forget for this reason.

At the end of the day, I had only recently removed a controlling man from my life, and I had zero interest in running the risk of inviting another one into my heart, let alone into my home to be around my children. To come out of one relationship with your heart broken in a million pieces, man, you better be prepared…

No one had warned me that by the time you turn 40, you start to get these hormones that kick in like crazy. Getting divorced at that age woke up some serious yearnings in me. I didn't want to get too serious with anyone while I was pouring all my energy into just getting to know myself again and getting my company going, but I was thinking, at this age, where do you even find men? I wondered why it couldn't be like that movie *Loverboy* – we order a pizza and the pizza guy shows up and really delivers. Ha ha! I am not ashamed to think or joke about that, hell men do it all the time and get away with it. I wish it was that easy.

All that time that I spent focused on one man, I was never imagining going through a divorce, nor ever thinking that I would ever be romantic with another man. With all the stress and the separate rooms we slept in, and the non-existent love life, I did have needs. I did want to have companionship and to be touched and be loved. But I couldn't just be with anyone that way. Still, I did eventually wind up having some… "experiences"… some good, some playful, some, well… whatever.

At first, during this whole new dating thing, it was kind of fun to discover that I can actually have sex and enjoy it and having a lot of orgasms. I had, after all, found myself in my 40's starting completely over and was now single learning this dating world. These gossiping people around who try to make it into a bad thing, when someone is starting all over again, can really just shove it. I am not ashamed, nor should any woman in my situation be ashamed, of trying to find yourself and trying to find a "yes" in all of this. That is as long as it is done the right way by all means.

My first "experience" was with a doctor, a really good friend I have known for several years. We had some good times but they never amounted to anything serious. Briefly after that, I started "dating" someone again, one of those things that happened naturally – he was younger than me, had never been married, didn't have any kids, and yet was very understanding of everything I had just been though. I had just come out of a marriage, sleeping in separate beds for years, and now that I just needed some affection from another human being. Anyone would. Not that I would just be with just anyone but with him, the most we could be to one another was essentially friends with benefits.

After all I had been through if I was going to be with a man, I needed a real man – a champion who is secure enough within himself to fly next to me with no worries, no games, and no drama. A man's got to lay the groundwork with me first if he wants to make it to any serious level with me. Where are those kind of men? I know one is out there somewhere – it's only a matter of him finding me. I don't have the time to hunt him down and I am not desperate at all but, I guess, I will surely keep my eyes open for him just in case. I am fine with myself and that is all that counts. Whatever comes naturally is what is best.

My sister sent me a text message during the first holiday season after the divorce was finalized, asking me, "What do you want for Christmas?" I replied, "Find me a real man. I'm sick of boys." I still find myself saying the same thing now. As I recall, while I was in Chicago with my family for Christmas at that time, I started getting several winks, emails from a dating match company. I started putting it all together and looked at my sister, like, "You didn't...!"

That was my first experience with anything like that. It just wasn't me at all. My sister said, "You said you wanted a man, so that's what I'm getting you!" I adore her sense of humor, but I had to close that account after getting all those "Hey Sexy" and "Hey Baby" messages. I mean, really?!

My friends had also been pushing me toward dating services, but I guess I'm just more traditional, just old-fashioned in a lot of ways. I'm really just a good girl. A lot of guys say that's very rare. I am not sure what others do, but I'm fine being me, set in my conventional ways. I tried a couple lunches with a dating service and the men I met just did not match anything that I was looking for, had the time for, or was interested in. I did however, meet some that have become good friends and I have a business relationship with today.

As I started to try this dating thing, I had to remember what it was even like to date. After hearing stories from my guy friends and even the from the "friends with benefits" guy, I had I learned about stuff they do, it was kind of like they were teaching me how to date. From the time I was 23 years old, my world had been my husband. I dated in high school and a little in college. I knew of some crazy stuff that people did and went through, but never imagined any of the craziness that is out there in the world today. Now, the dating world is apparently a whole different universe from what I knew and remembered. It's not easy, and it's not for sissies.

I now see that women are really selling out, giving everything away just for status or because of insecurity. I discovered that there are swingers and a people doing threesomes... I mean it all just sounded like pure madness to me.

After talking to my gynecologist and learning that there so many sexual transmitted diseases certainly out there, the whole game was changed for me. I still do not understand why the hell anyone would want to have sex unless they've been examined first. I guess this had been out there all along, but I was married and had never paid attention to it before. Post-marriage, I missed that whole AIDS era so I had never been part of that world. When you date, you have no idea if the person is clean or not.

After a couple of experiences and listening to all the stories out there, all that I was really interested in anymore was just getting back to normal. *Real* normal. I did not want to have so much pressure on me. At this point, I just could not muster up the energy that was needed to put into a relationship.

I needed all the energy I could muster to put into my business. I was waking up in the middle of their night at 2 a.m. because "someone upstairs" was waking me up with new ideas, convincing me that I had to make them all happen somehow. I had no more desire to date. I just wanted to focus on my children and my work as I was doing anyway. There was no room for any man in my life. I had too much left to handle and get figured out first.

I clearly remember, as I said before, a friend of mine one day asked me, "Why do people call it a mid-life crisis? Why can't it just be a life adjustment?" I think he was onto something. I had kept thinking to myself for years, *"There has to be more. Why can't there be more? Why is it so much to ask for someone to be supportive of my ideas and desires?"* That's all I needed, but I was certainly not ready to settle. I was not about to leap out there and commit to someone, the way I'd seen most women or men do, without taking the time to truly heal first. It was time for me to take some steps back.

I don't need a man to heal me. My passions lie in my children and my work, and I'm not jumping into anything that will expose either one of them to any craziness. It's not only a matter of being smart about it, but also a matter of trying to do what's right.

I explain to everyone that I am into doing the right thing – I am not into all this debauchery that I keep hearing about, and yet everyone seems to think that I'm the crazy one because I would rather have complete truth and integrity. I am not at all perfect but, friends tell me that I am asking for something impossible because I want a simple, safe, committed relationship built on respect, honesty, trust and absolutely no drama. They tell me that there really is no such thing, but I know there has to be someone out there like me. I won't give up hope.

Not just anyone will be allowed to come around my children. When I do find the right one, he will meet them eventually – but I am no dummy when it comes to my responsibility for my children and their emotional safety, and mine!

As I said, I am not at all desperate and I know that by the time I'm truly ready, I will never say never, it will happen. So, I'm in no hurry. In the meantime, I will not settle, but at least, I owe it to myself to breathe and I am getting my grove back.

Chapter 27:

For My Kids

Chapter 27: For My Kids

When I caught wind of a so-called "friend" of my ex-husband cooking for my children, taking them out, and buying them Christmas presents, I wasn't buying it and I wasn't having it.

If there was no romance then there was at least an interest – what woman brings her daughters around a man she hardly knows unless she is just plain reckless? On top of that, she was in the process of going through a divorce, so I didn't understand why she felt it was a good idea to take her children to play house with my ex-husband and my children, innocent or not.

With her began the real frustration and the journey to get through the aftermath of our divorce, including the "others" that may come in the form of her and future variations of her, further disrupting my new family dynamic.

I didn't care what my ex-husband did on his own time, but when it came to the time he was spending with my children, I had to demand respect for them and for myself.

When I requested to meet her so I could have a clearer understanding of who my children were beginning to spend so much time with, she accused me of being more confused than my children. She even accused me of feeling threatened by her. How delusional can you get? Why on earth would you have a problem with showing enough respect to acquaint yourself with the mother of two children you're spending increasing amounts of time around? The whole thing stunk and it irked me to no end.

My ex-husband didn't want me to meet her either. He wanted to know why he should have to seek approval of any of his friends through me, but that wasn't the point. The point was that, as their mother, I had a God-given right to know exactly who my children are spending time around. Period.

I wasn't buying the whole thing. If it was not romantic, it was surely at least emotional, but even that wasn't the point. She was with them many times while they were with their dad over summer vacation, she went with them to a Grizzlies game, and even went out for ice cream with them when I allowed a special one-night visit to give my son extra time with his father.

And what about her? With two young, impressionable girls to care for, in the midst of her own divorce, what was she doing bringing these girls around some strange man she was still getting to know?

After all I had been subjected to, having a P.I. trail me in search of strikes against my character to use to taint my image as a bad mother in the courts – suddenly we were bringing strange people of questionable character around our children like it was no problem? Unacceptable. From what I was able to learn about her, from the prominent showcasing of her nightlife across her social media wall, she was a teacher by day and a bar-frequenting Cougar by night – altogether it was strange that this woman was considered acceptable to bring around my children alongside the man who tried to spin my cranberry juice in a martini glass into some kind of cardinal sin that rendered me an unfit mother. It is very strange indeed since I was accused of being a drunk who did not care for my kids. It seemed that he was up to his old tricks again - back to bimbos, but I digress.

After I addressed my ex-husband with my concerns about her, he questioned our children about what they had told me. He had a "fatherly" talk with them, explaining to them that this woman was none of my business. Now I had a new bone to pick. I didn't like the way he was now putting my children in the middle of this.

We were just beginning to achieve some sense of balance and peace, so I wanted to figure out the right way to handle all that was going on in our lives *without* all the extra emotions and drama. Having this woman, or any woman for that matter, in the picture at this stage was not going to be much help to that effort.

After getting an approval from my attorney, I wrote her a message, telling her that I would like to meet her for coffee or lunch sometime.

She replied with thanks and expressed that she had enjoyed spending time with and getting to know my children. She told me what wonderful kids they were. To clear up any misconceptions, she "clarified" for me that she and my ex-husband were "simply good friends" and assured me nothing romantic was going on and that she was extremely respectful of my children and hers in this situation.

She "appreciated" and "understood" my concerns. *Hmmm…*

I elaborated to her that my children seemed to want for me to meet her. Now, I didn't think that was a horrible idea given that this woman was so often around my children, often buying presents for them. I figured, and said, that I expected her to understand my perspective as a mother. I informed her that my family was still healing and going through counseling – and that in that context, her relationship with him has caused some confusion for my children, inciting questions I wasn't prepared for about feelings they've encountered. I shared with her that it's clear to me that they don't tell my ex-husband everything, but they're still hoping for a different outcome. It is clear to me that they are still hurt and still healing and as their mother, it is a difficult thing for me to bear watching them go through such confusion.

It seemed like a red flag to me that my children wanted me to meet this woman – but my ex-husband did not.

It seemed a little strange to me, for another woman who I don't know to be buying clothes - she bought my daughter her first gymnastics outfit ... I mean, really?! - and many different gifts for my children. She was also cooking for them, and spending time with them that was supposed to be dedicated to quality time with their father during vacation, not dedicated to playing house with her while she cooks for my kids and my ex paints her fence. These are all things that were brought to my attention by my children after my son began wondering why his father never did that at our house. So there was a major concern on my side about all of this. I made sure that she knew I appreciated her kindness, but that it simply seemed odd, particularly since I didn't even know her, or knew anything about her, much less what the whole picture really was. As their mother, suddenly having no control over the elements they were surrounded by, made me very uncomfortable. It seemed irresponsible, like they were playing house with my children. I implored her to try and see things from my perspective, to try and understand.

I didn't want any drama. I didn't want to cause any issues. I simply wanted to meet her for an understanding of who my children were suddenly spending so much time with, someone they wanted me to like. I was not concerned about her dealings with my ex-husband. I was only concerned where my children were involved. She claimed that she understood my concerns as a mother, and that the healing process could be rough, especially since she was going through a divorce herself that had yet to be finalized. That, in itself, was a big red flag for me.

She had the nerve to tell me that she had not seen any indication of my children being confused about her friendship with my ex-husband – but she respected it if I said I did. To me, that just felt like an underhanded way of suggesting that she somehow knew my children better than I did, that I was mistaken. Strike. Then she went on to suggest that I seemed more confused than the children! Strike!

She issued a few more corrections to me, as she saw fit – that they do not "play house", that she wasn't even seeing them on a regular basis, that, yes, she had purchased small gifts for them on special occasions like birthdays and Christmas, but so had my ex-husband for her daughters... that there was no physical relationship between her and my ex-husband, and that there was therefore nothing in effect that should be perceived as odd. All of this, while she was going through a divorce herself. *Hmmm...*

According to her perspective and assessment, everything about it was "innocent and fun for all."

She really believed that I saw her as a threat, as an invader upon my territory, and pointed me, and my issues, in my ex-husband's direction, saying they needed to be taken up with him. She claimed to be just fine with getting together for a visit at some point with me, but I felt the need to question why my ex-husband had concerns about it.

I told her that my children seemed to like her, and that I was appreciative of her kindness toward them, that her responses indicated she had a good head on her shoulders – I felt that, given the similarity of our circumstances as divorced mothers with young children, she should be able to understand me and my position well.

I reiterated again that it would be nice to meet her one day, that I was not intimidated by her at all and invited her and a guest to our film premier for *Momo: The Sam Giancana Story* that was coming up the next week.

I joked with her that I believed my ex-husband's only concern about us getting together and chatting with one another was his fear that I would tell her the truth about him! She never made the plans to meet me, she simply said that she could not make it to the event, but she wished me luck.

I told my ex-husband if there was more to them than he was letting on, then they needed to figure out how to handle it like adults. I told him again, I have every right to know who the hell is around my children. Period!

After my ex finally decided to keep them away from her, she wrote to me and "requested" that I stop using her whenever I was frustrated with my ex-husband, insisting that neither she nor their relationship was any of my business. I have no idea what my ex was telling this woman but clearly it was drama at its best.

She claimed that out of respect for me she had distanced herself from my children – but that if my ex wanted to and was comfortable bringing them around her then that was his choice.

She had known him for nine months and she felt that she was in a position to tell me what was in his heart – that she knew, without a doubt, that he had the best interest of the kids at heart. That it was okay for her to be around my children.

She pointed out to me that we'd been divorced for a while, and that it was time for me to realize that he would date and move on to enjoy life and other relationships – just as she'd had to do with her ex-husband.

She had the gall to "inform" me that the healing process should *not* take as long as it seemed to be taking for me. Then, she shared with me the ultimate perspective – her divorce had been final "for a matter of weeks" and she had already moved on and "made great progress." Well, good for her! She had no idea who my ex really was and what the real picture was here. She clearly was not playing with a full deck of cards, but neither was my ex.

As a consolation, she assured me that I would always have the support of my ex-husband as far as a co-parenting relationship goes – but that I should expect to be disappointed if I expected anything more. I mean …really?!

She apologized if her honesty was hurtful. She was "simply tired" of hearing about how she was such a problem for me and my children, all words that came from my ex. Again, this was drama I did not need. Her final note she wrote in the message to me was, "Everyone deserves to be happy." How very sweet of her.

She wrote to me again, demanding that I not bring her or their relationship into the issues between him and me. I replied that most of this was not her business and she wrote to me "When it's my name involved, it IS MY BUSINESS." I could not believe this insanity, and I wrote her back to let her know if she continues to contact me I would seek further legal action. Her reply was "I see there is nothing more to discuss."

I copied everything and sent it to my attorney and my ex. I said "ENOUGH," I was about to bring out Mother Bear and tear this silly joke of a woman apart by contacting her ex-husband, the school she worked for and others. I wanted this to end! This woman was never to be allowed around my children, ever again! My counselor even agreed. This was bringing mental harm to them and it was not healthy for us to heal. I later found out that this woman's ex-husband was dating a 25 year old. I asked my ex-husband if he was such an complete idiot to bring this drama around our children and me? As if matters could get any crazier, I found out once I threatened legal action, that her divorce attorney was my attorney. I mean COME ON! I think my ex finally realized not to do this again, and not to put my children out to the wolves as I pleaded over and over. I had to get another attorney and, trust me, I got a good one. Talk about some stilettos, you got to wear some tall ones during a time like that. I just wanted to kick the ex with them and make sure they stuck up there for a long time. There is a lot more drama to this but I am getting too sick of even writing it to add any more. We got through it and lessons were learned but shame on him! In the end, my kids are never to be around her anymore and according to my ex he never "dated" her. He told me that he never even kissed her, as if I really care? All I know is, both of them were complete MENTAL CASES! Mother Bear is intact when needed. Did I ever say that forgiveness is not easy? It's not for sissies! Hell, I may be in the entertainment industry, but I am done with that drama and I am not about to create another Jerry Springer Show ... I have had enough!

I had enough of all the drama. I put my foot down hard in my stiletto. No more drama for me and no more for my kids!

Chapter 28:

Holding It All Together

Chapter 28: Holding It All Together

What held me together and kept me strong during the toughest of times was my children and my undying love for them. They were pure and their love was pure, so unlike much of the world I faced outside of them. If no one else knew the truth about who I was and how I was, they knew, and that was enough for me.

When I got a divorce, I was breaking up a family, but I wasn't the only one. I never wanted to worry about my children feeling like anything that happened between me and their father was their fault. I didn't want them to feel like anyone was abandoning them.

I knew that I had enough love in me that I was going to be okay, but I needed to make sure my kids were okay too.

I want my children to read this someday, to know and understand my truth. This is only my side of the story, and I want them to comprehend it as that and only that, no more and no less. I want them to understand how I thought and what I felt during those times that I know were confusing for them. I want them to understand the choices that I felt I had to make.

I want to be able to show my kids that it doesn't matter if you're adopted, or if you come from divorced parents, a so-called "broken" home, or anything else like that. Look at my life - I never knew my real father. I lived a while with a single mother. I lived for a while with my grandparents. Finally my mother met the man who became and remained my dad. There is always a light at the end of the tunnel, and things are whatever you make of them. Your life, in the end, becomes what you choose for it to be and it depends on how you handle what comes to you. All that other stuff, the mess, the distractions – that is not important.

It's all about what you do now to make things better and move forward. There were moments after the divorce when I ached with worry for my kids. How they were doing, how they were feeling, how they were taking all this – especially during the times when I didn't like the decisions I saw my ex-husband making. It's one thing when two married parents disagree on what's best for the children... but two bickering parents in the aftermath of a sloppy divorce? Fuhgedaboudit!

My children were not consulted about the hand they'd be dealt in life. They had not asked for any of this madness and chaos that comes with the world. They were dealt the cards that were dealt to them, and that became their lives. But I will do my absolute best to heal them and equip them. They deserved to have a family that could show them the meaning of values in this life, and those values included forgiveness. We are always learning, we are always healing, and we are always growing as a family.

To this day, we are still healing, one day at a time. It's been a few years, sure, but we are still overcoming, and I believe that there is finally a light shining on this family and we're going to be okay. There is almost a sense of balance and peace. They need him and they need me, that is the bottom line.

We've been seeing a counselor to help us find peace and to help us with the tools we need to really get this right. We just never know what lies ahead.

If he is strong enough to open his ears to his own heart, to get past all the ghosts of his past and their lingering demons, to not allow himself to be surrounded by horrible, miserable people that like to create turmoil between us, and step up like he should, then, I know that this family and its new dynamic will have a fighting chance.

We are in each other's lives forever. Our time spent as a couple of lovebirds has long come and gone, but we do remember the love we had at one time for one another, and the beauty of it all is, that we can still tap into that to form a strong team for our children. What I feel has happened, was basically all the anger surrounding us, mistrust between us, the attack of his mother, the world and his demons mixed with the craziness of his job.

Recently, he took us all out for a family dinner, and it felt so good to hang out together laughing with our kids again. It's just like with any family - you hate them sometimes, but you still love them. This is definitely an entirely different kind of love I have for him now— not a kind of love that everybody has in them, and not one that everyone is capable of understanding. But it's not meant for anyone to understand because it's my life and myself and my way. It's my path to my "yes." My "yes" is to repair this family and live the life I was meant to live.

Basically, right now, we're in a good place, and now that we are at a peace, we can see that we're still a family. He says that he's trying to do right by me. I say he should have been trying to do right from the beginning. Still I appreciate it. My kids are happy and that is what counts the most.

I realized that it did not and does not matter what he ever thought of or about me. It only matters what I think and know about myself, and that's the power my children will know because I will make sure that they have the right tools to learn from all this.

So if our ability to find our "yes," our peace, came through our divorce, then so be it. If it's what was best for our family, then so be it.

I hope he finds his yes as well and learns how to treat us all. How we treat each other.

Sometimes I brace myself, sure that it's bound to fall back apart. My counselor says that I shouldn't question anything – that I should just accept the good that's happening, but I can't help but to keep this one eyebrow up.

My children are such a blessing and, if I can just teach them everything I know now, they will have the tools to cope better down the road. Hopefully, I can give them the tools it took me years to understand and learn.

I begged him, which I hated, but I had to break through to him and get him to understand. I would grab him every once in a while, reminding him that, out of everyone, he should be able to understand what it's like having parents go through divorce and know that the things he was doing were selfish and wrong.

I also had to take a long, hard look at myself which is not an easy thing for anyone to do. I was no exception. But if you're going to heal and make a change, you've got to be the change you truly want to see in everyone and everything around you. I am holding it all together, in my titanium stilettos.

Chapter 29:

Truth and Integrity

Chapter 29: Truth and Integrity

Just in case going through the whole ordeal of my divorce and trying to pick up the pieces of a broken heart were not enough, life, being life and all, forced me to face yet another major hurdle.

At that time, in somewhat of a vulnerable stage, I had been left with pretty much no one that I could trust. Time revealed to me, slowly but surely, that anyone from neighbors, so-called friends, even mentors and associates supposedly rooting for me and helping me build my entertainment company were turning against me.

I had a vision of an entertainment powerhouse that would amount to something of the combined caliber of a Universal Studios, Time Warner, and STAX all under a single roof. Understanding that there was a lot I didn't know and still needed to learn in order to bring my vision to reality, I linked up with a wealth management professional who agreed to come on board as I built my business and act as a mentor, to guide me. He claimed that he wanted nothing from me or my company – only to see me succeed because he believed in me and everything I was striving for.

This wealth management "mentor" was introduced to me by my friend who thought that this man would be ideal to help me since he was part of an executive group that provided advice to other firms and individuals in business. His specialization was in wealth finance, so my friend thought he would have the acumen to help me put together a solid business plan – and since he was so active in the community, he'd have all the right connections to put me in front of valuable investors.

Meanwhile, he also agreed to take me on as a client to help me manage my money after my divorce. I signed an agreement with him that gave him permission to access information from my banks to help establish a budget for me, and more. What I did not do was have him sign an NDA – a Non-Disclosure Agreement – before turning over all my privileged information about my company and contacts. That little omission later hurt me in a big way.

I had trusted, foolishly, that since I was a client and he was a professional I thought I could trust him completely to conduct himself in a way that reflected and honored that relationship exactly. He had been so convincing with all his assurances that he would never cause harm to me or my company. I introduced him to my attorneys and I connected him with the rest of the team I had put in place to help me structure my company.

As I was introducing him to celebrities and many other well-known individuals who were successful in the industry, and those I built strategic partnerships with to help build my dream, he – behind my back – was busy convincing them to go another route and build an entirely separate company from my MVP3 Entertainment Group. A separate company, NewCo, the company he was pushing. It appeared to me that this NewCo was his real baby, and to nurture it, I felt he was coldly and callously trying to kill my company. He even tried to convince me and my other advisors that this was a better plan than my MVP3 vision.

When I asked my other advisors what they thought about this NewCo, many of them felt all this was a red flag. I then began to feel that my company was in danger of derailing.

As a matter of fact, that's almost exactly what happened. I felt that this man – the same man who had promised to help me manage my personal money, structure my company, and raise funds for my endeavors – was actually a very slick individual. He had managed to keep me busy with a wide array of tasks that he was "helping" me with. Meanwhile, I felt he worked his way through all of my contacts to build this NewCo, all along trying to convince them that his business venture was a better route than my own company, MVP3.

It was pointed out to me that, from him introducing me to some investment bankers who would help me structure a business plan and then direct me to the right investors to back the plan with capital, this guy had been able to tap into my entire vision until he had enough access to everything I had established to restructure and suit his own purposes. Even to this day, I think he and his cronies are still trying to secure capital to get this NewCo off the ground.

My ex-husband even had warned me and thought there were red flags as well – but after such a bitter divorce that had left us so distrustful of one another, I just suspected that my ex was sticking his nose into my business to keep trying to control everything, and just to find out if we were sleeping together (well that is what that bad mentor told me is why my ex called him), and basically keep all sorts of tabs on me, what I was doing, and who I was doing it with. It turned out, however, that my ex-husband really was trying to look out for me and protect me by making sure this man who was calling himself a mentor to me was not steering me wrong. In the end, the very man who was so angry at me because I divorced him wanted to protect me.

After I began questioning everything and becoming upset that I was not being included in meetings concerning my own business, the last draw came when this bad "mentor" was able to bypass me to talk to my attorney. It finally became more than crystal clear to me that this man I had trusted here in Memphis was actually, someone that was not in my best interest to do business with.

When I had the nerve to question this bad "mentor" and all his wrongdoings, he became defensive and responded that I was too emotional and did not know how to run a business. He then declared that he wanted nothing more to do with me or my company – as if I had any desire to continue any connection with him whatsoever anyway! He told me I should just go get a job and focus on taking care of my kids. He even de-friended me from his social media page. LOL !

In his words, it was not personal, only business. In my mind, I couldn't fathom any possible distinction. In the end, he had brought nothing to the table, but had stolen everything he could and had penetrated nearly the entire team I'd put so much sweat into building, the team of people I believed would stand by my side.

I felt like I couldn't trust anyone. I'd had to get away from the mean girls, the neighbors, and all the other crap that the divorce had stirred up. I reflected on all the games and trickery that had come with my divorce and my ex - his snake of an attorney, the P.I. detectives, my ex's boss being jailed for tax fraud while my ex had immunity. I was watching more and more people around me get fired for embezzling money from their companies. I was seeing more and more charities suffer while some person or business dipped into what was supposed to be allocated to their causes. I also watched so many people I knew encountering financial firms stealing money from them. It hit a lot of people in this city.

It was all too much, and I was getting fed up. It was like everyone in my midst had taken some kind of the worst "nightmare pill", and I was struggling to find the light in all this darkness closing in on me.

I swore to myself that my company would never be that way, and I would never employ or enable people who operated that way. I would never again have a marriage that wasn't based on truth, and I was not going to run a company based on anything but integrity. I wanted the real deal in everything. I had truly had enough.

I had to start all over again, get the right people behind my vision and I was focused on rebuilding to get people to trust in me that I would bring the right people to the table moving forward. I had to hire new attorneys. I am proud to say that I have some great attorneys now, but what an experience I had to go through and money I felt that was just wasted and lost.

I felt that everyone saw that I was divorced and assumed I was an easy target with easy money who was waiting to be taken advantage of. I knew I would have to strap on taller stilettos to be even stronger while I learned the best approaches to managing my money and providing for my children and keeping everything together while building this vision I had. I understood, then, more than ever, that building this empire would depend on strategic alliances with others who would truly enjoy seeing my dreams unfold just as much as I would.

I broke my titanium stilettos out of their glass case, put them on and got to work re-building my network in the industry – stomping new ground with a vengeance, kicking down doors in Nashville, Chicago, New York, and Los Angeles.

Life had given me another chance for a fresh start, and I would not rest until I found the right people who spoke my language and had a winning approach to anything they attached their names, time, energy, and effort to. People are used to hearing me speak this quote repeatedly: "You got sticks. I got a match. Together, we can go make a fire!"

Coming together with other producers, writers, and directors to accomplish what others dismiss as impossible has been a tremendous blessing that I will never take for granted. I know it's not easy for people to break through the initial fear, doubt, and "What's in it for me?" mentality to instead see the win–win in the opportunities I am bringing forth – but those who do realize that together, with our combined visions and passions and abilities, we can change not only our communities but also the face of the entire industry.

I am on a mission by building not only a home of my own but also a company of my own, the best way I know how, on a solid foundation of truth and integrity. As I try my best to teach my kids the same values of truth and integrity that I strive to instill within my company, I demand of myself that I be a prime example of those values in action, every day I try without fail.

I am not perfect but …one "yes" at a time.

Afterward:

The Making of an Empire

Afterward: The Making of an Empire

I remain focused on my mission to build an entertainment powerhouse. I know that I can and I will. I am determined, and I know I have enough energy and knowledge from all I've experienced. Now I have no fear. I will build an empire, and my legacy, on such solid ground that I know they will both stand strong. Richard Sandor did it, Fred Smith did it, Bill Gates did it, Steve Jobs did it, and so can Marie Pizano.

Cocky? No – just backed with confidence and perseverance. I am maintaining the right connections, the vision, the energy, and the gumption to remain strong and unstoppable as I go for my dreams and watch them take the shape of reality.

On this journey, I've had countless ups and downs, many trials and tribulations, but each one just brings me closer to finding that "yes." Already in place, I have a film company, a music publishing company, and a talent management company all under one umbrella – so far, so good, I'd say. Now, I just have to keep my stilettos pointed and moving in the right direction.

Isaac Hayes once said, "Know the business, learn the business, own something," and I took heed. That's what I'm doing today, and it's what I'll be doing tomorrow and ever after – sissies need not apply!

As for my present situation, I am now in a good place with so much appreciation for every bit of all that it has taken for me to get here.

Through friends of mine in the entertainment industry, I was introduced to Morgan Freeman. I felt we hit it off as kindred-spirits right from the start. He is very kind, funny and wise. During one of our visits, we went golfing and had dinner with a group of our mutual friends. Morgan and I shared one of our "war-stories" with each other. When I told him about my motorcycle accident that I had when I was younger, and showed him the "T" scar on my leg, he said, "The "T" is not for Tennessee, It is for Tough." From the moment he said that, I felt a power inside and with a big smile on my face, I said, "You know what Morgan, I like you!" And from that moment, Morgan's words gave me a new way to look at that "T" on my leg. He was right, he reminded me, I am tough, and I can beat the odds, stand tall and go live my life the way it was meant for me to live, even with this scar or any scars for that matter.

Not too long after that dinner with Morgan Freeman, I made a big decision for my children and I, to move into a new home, a fresh start in a new place, one that we can make our own for now, one that I can decorate to reflect myself and my own tastes, one where I can leave dishes in the sink overnight and laundry in the basket if I choose – and most importantly, one that, my children are happy in.

I have found a state of peace with my ex-husband that at one time, I never imagined we could achieve. We are doing an amazing job together, juggling the kids and balancing the forward movement of our own separate lives and newfound forgiveness. Our health is intact, and our children have smiles on their faces.

I have established a new set of positive friends and neighbors. I have amassed a great team that stands by my side and puts genuine effort into helping me build my company and to bringing my dreams – our dreams – to fruition. I have wonderful, knowledgeable, insightful advisors who have proven to have my best interests at heart. My mentor, Richard Sandor, remains my rock star and continues to point me in the right direction to help make me a success. I have many advisors that have joined in to help me succeed as well. The people I have in my corner are powerful business figures, as well as, movers and shakers within my industry, and they believe in me. I even had one of my most special dreams come true when I got to meet Mr. Fred Smith, Founder of FedEx Corporation – a meeting and a day that I will always treasure.

My team and I are in the midst of kicking off a singer/songwriter showcase in efforts to highlight the musicians I represent out of Memphis and to really give back to this city, helping bring an opportunity about for these local musicians. I recently signed some new artists, giving them publishing and distribution deals and taking them under my wing. Now we're well on the way to having their songs released all over the country.

My film, *Momo: The Sam Giancana Story* has, to date, won 3 awards for "Best Documentary," the film was picked up in a few countries overseas and will be released nationally and available on DVD. And as I write this, I am in development on a few films and I just completed producing a stage play, that opened in Memphis. I am also in the middle of working with police and retired FBI to get all the facts I need for the film I will be producing based on a true story called, *Echoes of Shannon Street.*

I have planted my seeds and I continue to water them attentively, as I revel in watching them bloom, a lot of that drama has dissipated and I am finally feeling I have healed in many ways. There comes challenges financially with running a company and being a single mother but, finally, I can breathe. Finally, it is all coming together. Finally, I am comfortable in my own skin. I am open to love. I am taking in all that life has to offer. Just seeing happiness in my children is such a joy and peace that helps me through everything and makes me smile. Finally, my ex-husband and I are making it work in the dynamic we have now. There are still some challenges but we are finding our way through the storm.

Every day a new door opens, and a new opportunity presents itself. Every moment of my life feels truly amazing to me. I am living, breathing proof, alive and in living color, that if you set out to do something, and you believe in yourself, staying committed to doing the right things, then your dreams can come true.

As I regularly remember my mom saying, "I picked up my panties and moved on," the words of my dad also come to mind, him saying, "Kid, what works for me is not going to work for you," and "It's not all about love. It's about what you can handle." I reflect often on the past several years of my life, all that's been presented to me and all that I've endured. I realize that, by bearing it all, I have defeated my fears, embraced my scars, and bolstered my confidence. I love what I do, and I am ready to handle anything that life throws my way.

Every day I am going full speed, finding and nearing another "yes." Walking tall in my stilettos, boldly facing the journey ahead and hurdling over the "good ol' boy" network. I am on a mission.

I have never taken "no" for an answer, and there's no way I'm about to start now. I know there will be more hurdles to leap past and more doors to kick down, yet, I am mindful and thankful, always, of the ones that fly right open as though expecting me before I even have a chance to knock.

There is no turning back for me. I see nothing as a failure. With a deep breath, I leap off of a cliff every day, and I land standing tall every time. I feel much like I did before that motorcycle accident derailed what I thought was supposed to be my future – like that invincible girl, unstoppable, full of ideas, fueled by passion and possessing the ability to do it all.

At the end of the day, it's all about trying your hardest to do your best and to be your best so you will establish roots on a solid foundation.

I'm taking one step at a time in my stilettos, reminding myself of all the time put in and the trials that have gone into perfecting my stride and my strut – reminding myself, as I step closer to my dreams, that the ride of life has more in store for me and it is not for sissies.

But, I CAN and I WILL go find my "yes".

About the Author

Marie Pizano is a native Chicagoan. Since moving to Memphis in 1999, she has fondly called the Bluff City home. She has served on several charitable organizations in different capacities, she was a member of the International Children's Foundation and the Women's Foundation for Greater Memphis, and of the Commission on Missing & Exploited Children. She is also the co-founder of the Tiara Tea Society and was the Chair for Go Red for Women. Most importantly, Marie is a full-time, hands on mother of two.

Pizano started her own entertainment business known as MVP3 Entertainment Group.

MVP3 acts as the umbrella organization that includes JND Films, UROC Records/Publishing and Zazu & Valentina talent management agency. She has had experience as an actor and a model, has been a co-producer of a local TV shows in Memphis and is the creator and Producer of "Girls Night Out" with award-winning producer Steven Boyle. She is an Executive Producer of the award-winning, history-changing documentary, "MOMO: The Sam Giancana Story." As the CEO of MVP3, Pizano is helping guide the careers of musical talent, producers, film directors, writers, actors and so much more. Her passion and commitment is focused on building MVP3 Entertainment Company founded on solid ground, truth and integrity and she sees a powerful need to use music and film to help to advance communities forward. Recently she launched a YouTube web series called, "The MVP3 TV SHOW: The Making of an Empire." She is currently in the process of developing a few film projects which will excel her plans to help fuel economic growth throughout the Tennessee and Delta area while also on a mission to become Globally known as a leading entertainment powerhouse. The rights to her book, "From Barefoot to Stilettos, it's not for sissies" have been licensed to JND Films. The film version, based on her story, is now currently now in the development stages. For more information on her companies you can visit www.MVP3media.com, and www.FromBarefootToStilettos.com

About the Artist

Michael P. Maness is an eclectic Mid-South Artist that sees ART in everything, everywhere. His vision evokes his peculiar view of the world; BRIGHT, COLORFUL, and interesting, with a dash of hope.

Since the age of 8 Mike has constantly been drawing, painting, designing, or writing for somebody. From limited edition posters to album covers, and movie posters, for over 30 years he has been in the business of art, advertising, and marketing. Michael has contributed stories and illustrations to regional and national magazines and has also worked for many Fortune 500 companies.

Mike's latest venture is his acclaimed "Song Series" in which he has worked with some of the greatest songwriters of the past 50 years. This list includes, Rock and Roll Hall of Famer, Steve Cropper, and his songs, including "Sitting on the Dock of the Bay", Larry Weiss, who wrote the multi-platinum song "Rhinestone Cowboy" which now on display in the Tennessee State Museum, and Mark James who wrote the Elvis Presley smash hit, "Suspicious Minds".

In 1997, Michael was diagnosed with Lymphoma and Bone Marrow cancer. A bone marrow transplant not only got his health back on track, but his brush with death also gave him a new attitude and perspective on life along with a new vigor that took over the direction of his craft. His unique style and iridescent colors are indicative of his new passion for life and his unique interpretation of his surroundings.

"I see the world from a different angle than most people," says Maness. "Instead of a constantly changing world, a crowd doing the expected; I paint the individual and focus on the individual's spirit to tell a story."

Three bouts with Cancer and a brush with Congestive Heart Failure later, Mike's generous donations of original paintings and prints have raised over four million dollars for St. Jude Children's Research Hospital, the Red Door, Clay Walker's Band Against MS, The International Children's Heart Foundation, The Blues Foundation, The Susan G. Komen Foundation and over 150 other organizations.

Mike's awards are numerous, including the "Keeping the Blues Alive" award from the International Blues Foundation, "Best of the Best" in his home county in Mississippi, and the "Memphis Hero" award from the Orpheum Theater in Memphis, Tennessee.

Mike's work can viewed at http://www.artbympm.com Michael P. Maness is now living in Southaven, Mississippi.

About the Photographer

Hal Jaffe is a second generation photographer. He has a reputation of creating quality portraits and commercial photography for very reasonable prices. Within a few years of opening his first studio, Jaffe Studio, Hal Jaffe personally photographed approximately. 7500 sittings, mostly children and also a lot of family groups. Whether photographing celebrities such as famous actors and actresses in the entertainment industry, government officials, a child or family portraits. Hal has the experience and knowledge to create a portrait that will be cherished for a lifetime. As a professional photographer, Hal uses his extensive knowledge of lighting and posing to create portraits that show the beauty and personality of the subject to be cherished for many generations to come.

You can view his photography at www.haljaffe.com.

Jaffe Studio is a nationally award winning portrait studio located in Memphis, Tennessee.

Jaffe Studio
4902 Poplar Ave
Memphis, TN 38117
901-682-7501

About Robin Cooper / The Exodus Foundation, Inc.

A portion of the proceeds of this book are donated to The Exodus Foundation, Inc.

Coming from the Turner Circle projects of <u>Forrest City, Arkansas</u>, it would have been very easy for Robin L. Cooper to succumb to her environment and become just another statistic. Robin was born on May 19, 1966, as the only child of Mrs. Louella Payne-Gardner and the late Mr. L. J. Sain. She attended Forrest City High School and graduated from Crowley's Ridge Technical Institute in 1984, where she received her Business diploma.

A product of a single mother home, Robin yearned for the love that a young girl would normally receive from her father. Her search for that love led her into the first of many situations that would shape her life and, ultimately, her destiny. Robin became the victim of what is now called domestic violence, becoming entangled for many years before the shackles were broken. She was determined that she would not allow herself or anyone else to suffer the humiliation and sense of powerlessness that comes with being a victim of domestic violence.

In 2009, graduating cum laude, she received her Bachelor of Science degree in Bible and Theology from Crichton College, now Victory University, in Memphis, TN. While pursuing her undergraduate degree, she zealously began to share her acquired knowledge with others. In 2007, she was hired as the first instructor for Daughters of Zion All Women Bible College in Memphis, TN. During this time, she taught Bible and Church History, Basic Theology, Theology Proper, Prophets, the Gospels, and other subjects. She is currently pursuing her Master of Science in Mental Health Counseling.

Upon completing her studies and graduating from Crichton College, she did not rest on her laurels and consider her journey complete; rather, she had a vision of an organization designed to help others come out of the torment through which she personally walked for nearly two decades. She began to pray, to prepare, to plan, and to design what is now <u>The Exodus Foundation, Inc.</u>

The Exodus Foundation, Inc., a non-profit 501(c)(3) corporation, was envisioned in 2003 and manifested in 2010. Throughout the seven years prior to the organization's inception, Ms. Cooper engaged in extensive research on domestic violence. During this time, she interviewed numerous victims, survivors, law enforcement officials, and experts in her quest to acquire the knowledge, information, and resources necessary to bring public awareness and prevention to domestic abuse. For more information please visit www.exodusfoundationdv.org

Advertisements

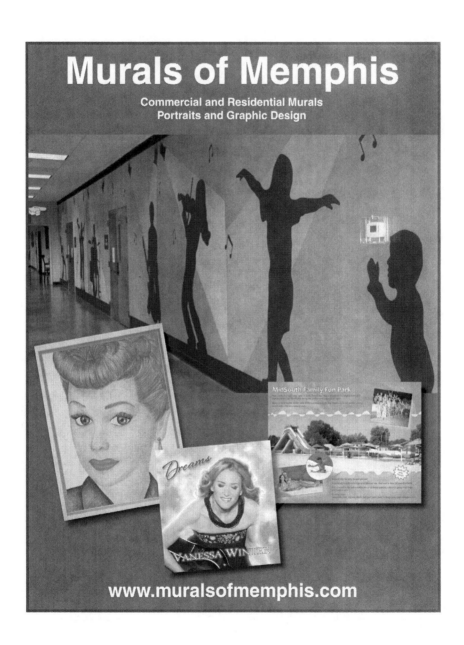

DANIEL SHAY'S
A HAIR STUDIO

danielshays.com

Daniel & Shay Gomez
Owner Stylists

Karl Smith
Stylist

Let's Talk About Fitness!

Finally Fit Memphis
Dedicated to helping individuals accomplish their *FITNESS* and *NUTRITION* goals!

Finally Fit Programs
Private (1:1) | Semi-private (3:1) | Group training (5+)

Nutrition Nanny program is offered for only private and semi-private individuals.
Mobile training as well as studio facility available for all clients, YOU choose your fitness destination :-)

FITNESS ASSESMENT TAKEN
Weight | Height | Measurements | BMI | Body
Fat lbs % | Body water %

901.219.1070
www.finallyfit-memphis.com

Heavenly Hands

Specializing in:

Swedish Massage

Deep Tissue

Reflexology

Private Events & More

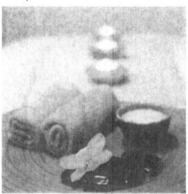

Experience A Touch of Heaven

Ronnie Leavy, LMT
Booking by Appointment only
heavenlyhands2u@yahoo.com

**FIVE TIME NATIONAL AWARD
WINNING THERAPIST**

**VOTED THERAPIST OF THE
YEAR 2006**

MVP3 ENTERTAINMENT GROUP
FILM * MUSIC * COMMUNITY
www.MVP3media.com

FOR MORE INFORMATION ON OUR
UPCOMING FILMS, MUSIC or
COMMUNITY/Charitable PROJECTS
CONTACT
Showcase@MVP3media.com

Let's Come Together to make films and music happen!

www.militarywarriors.org

CPSIA information can be obtained at www.ICGtesting.com
Printed in the USA
LVOW13s1809261213

366960LV00001B/3/P